I Hate to Burst
Your Bubble, But…

Things You Thought
Were True
But Really Aren't

Dave Guthmann

Table of Contents

Preface

You may have seen several of the "common misconceptions" that appear in this book. You know what they are—"facts" a lot of people believe, but actually aren't true. There's a good chance you've watched TV's "Mythbusters" debunk various popular beliefs. You've probably seen some of these false facts in one of those "viral" emails everyone in the world seems to forward on to everyone else in the world. You might be a fan of Snopes.com, an excellent website that sets the record straight about popular urban legends and rumors. Or you might have looked at one of several excellent books that debunk common misconceptions, e.g., David Diefendorf's Amazing...But False! Hundreds of "Facts" You Thought Were True, But Aren't.

Awhile back, I decided to keep a file of these on my computer. My collection quickly grew. I started to look for new ones hidden in a variety of spots on the Internet and in the printed world. I realized I had quite a collection—worth sharing with others who find this stuff intriguing.

My next step was to fact-check these "non-facts." Just like certain truths could be revealed as untruths, it was certainly possible some supposed "myths" might actually be true. For example, I ran across the claim that commercial airlines were wasting your time with water landing instructions—these landings were virtually impossible. However, US Airways pilot Sully Sullenberger proved it was possible—at least on the Hudson River! Another supposedly debunked myth was cell phones don't really mess up the navigational systems of airplanes. But more detailed research suggested the jury is still out on that one, so I tossed that one too.

So why is my personal collection of interest when several of these misconceptions are available elsewhere? Three reasons:

1) You'll find more misconceptions, myths, etc. here than any of the other sources for this kind of stuff—I have no doubt you'll learn some things you didn't know,

1

2) Hopefully, you'll enjoy the "user-friendly" short bullet form I used—with no long essays, this is the kind of book you can take to the bathroom and enjoy, and

3) I published it on the cheap—it may not have the wonderful graphics of those books available at Amazon.com and your book store, but it sure is less expensive.

One caveat: doing it on the cheap means no money spent on proofreaders and the like. All errors are completely and utterly mine. If you find some glaring error, you only have me to blame.

And, as always, thank you to my lovely wife Diane not only for providing lots of helpful suggestions, but for putting up with the time I spent on this project.

I hope you enjoy what follows. I'm guessing you will soon notice how often these untruths are spouted as gospel. No doubt you'll get a kick out of knowing that "common wisdom" is not all that it is cracked up to be.

And if you're so inclined, you'll be in a better position to burst a few bubbles yourself!

American History

Not all colonists supported the fight for **American independence**. John Adams estimated one-third were in favor, one-third were opposed, and one-third didn't care.

The population of **American Indian tribes** was not devastated by warfare with white settlers. Diseases these settlers brought from Europe (small pox, measles, cholera, etc.) nearly wiped Native Americans out.

The **Battle of Bunker Hill** was not fought on Bunker Hill. It was fought on nearby Breed's Hill.

Contrary to the all-white casts in most movie Westerns, **black cowboys** were common in the Old West. It's estimated one of every three cowboys was black.

John Wilkes Booth wasn't the only offender who died as a result of Abraham Lincoln's assassination. Four of his co-conspirators were hanged within three months of the assassination.

The **Boston Tea Party** was not a protest against high taxes. In fact, the protest occurred after the Tea Act of 1773 lowered prices—British tea was actually cheaper than smuggled tea. Some tax remained, so there's no doubt some protesters were still upset over "taxation without representation." However, an equally important concern was the Tax Act would put smugglers out of business—a problem because many of the smugglers were colonists.

Though many have stated the U.S. was founded on **Christian principles**, this is not the case. The Constitution does not mention God. And the 1796 Treaty of Tripoli, signed by President John Adams, states, "The Government of the United States is not, in any sense, founded on the Christian Religion."

Christopher Columbus did not discover the area we now know as the United States of America. He never even set foot on mainland North America. He landed on several Caribbean islands and South America in the 1490s.

The U.S.'s battle against **communism** did not begin after World War II. In 1918, the United States sent over 3000 troops into Russia to fight against the Bolshevik revolutionaries.

Though films and books suggest **cowboys** ruled the West well into the 20th century, they really only had a significant impact until the 1880s. Homesteading and railroads replaced the cowboy as a major force in the West in the late 19th century.

No **General Custer** died at the battle of Little Bighorn. Custer had been demoted to Lieutenant Colonel ten years earlier, so he died as Lieutenant Colonel Custer.

Confederate President **Jefferson Davis** did not try to escape wearing women's clothes. He was wearing his own clothing when captured, but hastily grabbed his wife's cloak as he voluntarily surrendered to Union soldiers.

Other than John Hancock, the members of the Continental Congress did not sign the **Declaration of Independence** on July 4, 1776. It was signed on August 2 by most delegates, and in the following months by the latecomers.

Abraham Lincoln's **Emancipation Proclamation** did not free any slaves. It only referred to the slaves in the Confederate states, and those states just ignored the order.

When Admiral **David Farragut** said in the Civil War, "Damn the torpedoes—full speed ahead!" he was not referring to torpedoes as we know them. At the time, "torpedoes" referred to underwater mines, i.e., beer kegs filled with gunpowder.

There is no evidence any women burned their bras as part of the **feminist movement** in the 1960s. At the 1968 Miss America contest, protesters threw several items, including bras, girdles, and makeup, into trash cans, but no bras were burnt.

The French and Indian War was not between the French and Indians. During America's colonial period, the British and the colonies fought against the French and their American Indian allies.

Abraham Lincoln did not write the **Gettysburg Address** on the back of an envelope on the train trip to Gettysburg. He started composing and rewriting several weeks beforehand and no envelopes were involved.

Mrs. O'Leary's cow did not start the **Great Chicago Fire** of 1871. The story was fabricated by a news reporter looking for an interesting spin on the story.

Horace Greely was not the first to say, "Go west, young man." Newsman Greely was just quoting a fellow named John Soule.

During the **Gulf of Tonkin incident**, which led to a major deployment of U.S. forces in Vietnam, North Vietnamese ships did not attack U.S. ships without provocation. President Johnson told congress it was an unprovoked attack, but a National Security Agency report has since revealed the incident was deliberately distorted, i.e., U.S. ships shot first.

President **William Henry Harrison** did not die because he didn't wear a coat while giving a long inauguration speech in the cold. Harrison didn't get sick until three weeks after his inauguration. Besides, studies have shown exposure to the cold doesn't make you sick.

Nathan Hale's last words weren't "I only regret that I have but one life to give for my country." They were "It is the duty of every good officer to obey any orders given him by his commander-in-chief."

Though the famous film of the horrifying explosion suggests otherwise, not everyone died in the **Hindenburg** disaster. Sixty-two of the ninety-seven passengers somehow survived.

The **Hindenburg** disaster was not a result of the ship's hydrogen gas catching fire. The outside of the ship had been treated with aluminum powder—now a common ingredient in rocket fuel. It was the ship's skin that ignited so quickly.

The United States did not gain **independence** in 1776. The colonies only declared their intent to become independent. The American Revolution did not officially end until 1783, and the United States wasn't officially a federal union until 1789.

The famous photograph of the U.S. flag being raised on **Iwo Jima** does not show the actual event. It shows a reenactment. The first raising of the flag was not captured on film.

The Presidency of **John F. Kennedy** wasn't associated with "Camelot" during his tenure in office. While the Broadway musical was popular during his Administration, the strong association developed after his assassination. In an interview only a week after his death, wife Jacqueline described President Kennedy's love for the musical. The Camelot parallel spread as the nation mourned his death.

Though **General Robert E. Lee** led the Confederate Army during the Civil War, he believed slavery was immoral and the southern states should not secede from the Union.

Contrary to popular belief, the **Liberty Bell** was not a particularly cherished piece of property in the early years of the country. It was sold as scrap metal in 1828 at a discount rate, but the deal fell through when the purchaser decided it wasn't worth the effort.

The **Liberty Bell** did not crack while commemorating American independence on July 4, 1776. It cracked while ringing for the funeral of Chief Justice John Marshall in 1835.

Abraham Lincoln did not support the Civil War as a means to abolish slavery. Soon after the war started, Lincoln said, "My paramount object in this struggle is to save the Union, and is not either to save or destroy slavery."

Sitting Bull did not lead the 1876 battle against Custer at **Little Bighorn**. Crazy Horse was the war chief who led the battle. As head chief, Sitting Bull stayed behind to protect the camp.

The sinking of the **Lusitania** in 1914 did not directly lead to U.S. involvement in World War I. The U.S. didn't enter the war until 1917.

Peter Minuit did not purchase **Manhattan** from the Canarsee Indians for $24. No money was exchanged. Some items, e.g., trinkets, were exchanged, but no known record exists.

There was never a Civil War battle between the **Monitor and the Merrimac**. The Merrimac was severely damaged many years before and renamed the Virginia before its battle with the Monitor.

The great **New York City blackout** of 1965 did not lead to an increase in the birthrate nine months later. The rate was similar to previous rates at that time of the year.

The United States was not the first country to allow women to vote when it ratified the **19th Amendment** in 1920. That honor goes to New Zealand, which did it 27 years earlier.

The battleship U.S.S. Constitution, known popularly as **Old Ironsides**, was not made of iron. It was made of wood.

Pennsylvania was not named for its founder, William Penn. The King of England named it in honor of Penn's father, Sir Admiral William Penn.

The **Pilgrims** who landed on the Mayflower in 1620 were not the first English settlers in North America. Jamestown in Virginia, and many other settlements, were established as early as 1607.

The folks on the Mayflower did not refer to themselves as **Pilgrims**, nor did anyone else at the time. It wasn't until an 1820 bicentennial ceremony that anyone referred to them as Pilgrims.

The **Pilgrims** did not wear mostly black clothes, with big buckles and black steeple hats. This image was formed by writers in the 19th century when that look was associated with prim and proper religious folk.

General **William Prescott** likely did not say, "Don't fire until you see the whites of their eyes," to American soldiers at the 1775 Battle of Bunker Hill. But if he did say it, he wasn't the first. Scotland's Andrew Agnew said it in 1743 at the battle of Dettingen.

Though the capital of Virginia is named after him, and he did advocate settlement in America, **Sir Walter Raleigh** never traveled to the area we now know as the United States. He did make it to Newfoundland and South America, but he never came anywhere near Virginia.

Paul Revere did not warn citizens in Concord that the "British are coming." He was detained by the British and a fellow named Samuel Prescott did it. Longfellow's erroneous poem helped build Revere's undeserved reputation.

During the **Revolutionary War**, American soldiers had no advantage over British soldiers in terms of non-traditional warfare, e.g., surprise attacks and hidden ambushes. The British used these techniques as often as the Americans. And Americans used the conventional "line of soldiers" approach just as often as the British.

Betsy Ross did not sew, or otherwise create, the first American flag. This completely fictitious story was made up by her grandson nearly 100 years after the introduction of the flag.

People believed to be witches in **Salem** were not burned at the stake. They were hanged.

While the **San Francisco earthquake** of 1906 caused many deaths and tremendous damage, it wasn't the direct cause of most of the city's damage. The fire that followed caused considerably more deaths and property damage.

Scalping did not originate with American Indians. It originated in Europe, and was introduced to the Indians when white colonists offered a reward for the scalp of other Indians.

The Rough Riders did not fight on horseback during the **Spanish-American War** in Cuba, and were not led by Teddy Roosevelt. While trained to ride on horses, they left their horses behind. And they were led by Colonel Leonard Wood. Roosevelt was second in command.

Despite many famous paintings, no Americans fought under the **Stars and Stripes** flag during the Revolutionary War. The first time American soldiers fought under this version of the flag was the Mexican-American War in 1846.

The suicide rate did not change after financiers supposedly jumped out of windows during the 1929 **stock market crash**. There was no difference in suicide rates before and after the crash.

Though gold was discovered in California in 1848 on land owned by **John Sutter**, Sutter did not die rich. He was originally granted the land by the Mexico government, but it was lost to squatters when the U.S. Supreme Court ruled his claim was invalid.

The American settlers who fought for **Texan independence** in 1836 did not have a reasonable claim for land that belonged to Mexico. They didn't like paying property tax and they were upset with Mexico's decision to outlaw slavery.

The compromise in the U.S. Constitution that counted blacks as **3/5 of a person** was not a result of Southern states refusing to count blacks as whole people. The South, with its large number of slaves, wanted to count blacks as whole people so their overall population, and their congressional representation, would be greater. Because they had few slaves, the North wanted to exclude blacks completely.

No man dressed as a woman so he could enter a lifeboat as the **Titanic** sank. There's some evidence fellow survivors threw a shawl over a young man's head after he had already entered the lifeboat; however, no man wore a dress as commonly seen in movies about the Titanic.

Tomahawks were not thrown by Indians in battle. They wouldn't want to lose this valuable possession, so it was only used as a club.

Though western migration on **wagon trains** was very dangerous and often fatal, Indians were not the greatest threat. In fact, of the over 300,000 deaths that occurred on wagon trains, less than 400 were the result of Indian attacks.

The **War of 1812** didn't begin and end in 1812. It wasn't over until 1815.

Animal Kingdom

No **alligators** have ever been found in the New York sewer system. There are plenty of rats, however.

Ants aren't busy all of the time. They work only about one-fifth of their life. They only seem busy because the ant colony as a whole stays busy throughout the day.

Contrary to the song "Home on the Range," no **antelope** "play" in North America. Antelope are only found in Africa and Asia. The animals mistakenly called antelopes in North America are pronghorn sheep.

Most species of **armadillos** don't roll into a ball when attacked. Only a South American species relies on this defense. North American armadillos escape predators by running away or digging into the ground.

The **Australian Shepherd** dog did not originate in Australia. It originated in California.

Despite being the symbol of the U.S., the **bald eagle** isn't a particularly noble creature. Bald eagles have been known to steal puppies and even attack people.

Bald eagles aren't bald. "Balded" was a Middle English term for "white."

The **Baltimore oriole** was not named after the city of Baltimore. First the bird, and then the city, were named after Lord Baltimore.

Bats are not blind. Their use of sound detection, i.e., echolocation, improves night activity, but they also use their eyesight.

Though you often hear the term "bear hug," **bears** don't hug. The closest thing resembling a hug is when a bear holds its victim while tearing the victim with its teeth.

Bears don't hibernate. They become "dormant," similar to sleeping. Their temperature, heart rate, and breathing don't slow like a true hibernator.

Beavers don't use their tails to tamp down mud while building dams. They will, however, slap their tails on the water's surface to warn other beavers of danger.

Bees do not collect honey. They collect nectar, which is processed into honey by the bee hive.

The phrase, "eat like a **bird**" is a misnomer. Most birds will eat anywhere from 25% to 50% of their body weight in a given day. Humans generally eat the equivalent of only about 1% to 2% of their weight each day.

Birds do not turn their heads frequently in reaction to sounds. They move their heads to improve their vision. It's easier for them to turn their necks than move their eyes.

Mother **birds** don't reject their chicks if handled by a human being. They don't smell well enough to even know if a human touched their chick. That claim likely spread to deter people from picking up chicks that have fallen from their nest. The real reason you should leave them alone is falling is part of the natural process of learning to fly.

Bloodhounds aren't called that because they smell blood to track humans. The name comes from the tradition of keeping breeding records, which document their "bloodlines."

Boa constrictors don't crush their victims to death. They constrict the breathing of their victims, causing them to suffocate.

The blue whale, the world's biggest animal, is not the world's longest animal. The longest is the **bootlace worm**, which grows to 200 feet—twice as long as a blue whale.

Buffalo never roamed the prairies of North America. Those were bison. They were mislabeled because they reminded Europeans of water buffalo from Asia and Africa.

Camels do not carry water in their humps. They do, however, use the fat stored in their humps to survive long periods without water.

Camels were not originally from Africa or Asia. They originated in North America. Millions of years ago, they crossed the Bering land bridge into Asia and on to Africa. They later died out in North America.

Milk is not good for **cats**. Most cats are lactose-intolerant, and experience an upset stomach when they drink milk.

Cats don't rub against your leg as a sign of affection. They are marking their territory with their odor, letting other cats know you are their property.

No **cat** has ever killed a sleeping baby by sucking the baby's breath. This rumor grew when a cat was found next to a dead baby; however, the actual cause was sudden infant death syndrome.

Cats do not always land on their feet. While they have an inbuilt automatic twisting reaction that helps them do that, it's not always possible in short falls.

Catgut, used for making stringed instruments, does not come from **cats**. It generally comes from sheep or horses.

Centipedes rarely have 100 legs. They can have anywhere from 28 to 354.

There is no such creature as a **Cheshire cat**, nor was it originated by Lewis Carroll in <u>Alice's Adventures in Wonderland</u>. The name comes from "grin like a Cheshire cat," an expression of unknown origin popular before Carroll wrote his book.

The **chicken** is not considered a flightless bird. Chickens can fly a little bit, though the longest recorded flight was only 13 seconds.

Snake charmers don't entrance **cobras** with music. Cobras are deaf and only respond to the movements of the snake charmer and his flute.

Cockroaches are not the most likely survivors of a nuclear war. Tests have shown cockroaches would be one of the first insects to die.

Cold-blooded animals don't always have cold blood. Unlike warm-blooded animals, which keep a constant temperature regardless of the weather conditions, the temperature of cold-blooded animals varies. It can be very high in hot environs.

It's not true **cows** can't walk down stairs. They can be led up or down stairs.

Crickets don't chirp by rubbing their legs together. They rub their wings together.

Crocodiles don't cry crocodile tears. They don't even have tear ducts.

Not all **crows** are black. For example, Brazil's crimson fruit crow is bright red.

The term **daddy longlegs** does not refer to a specific creature. It's a nickname for three different arthropods: the crane fly, the cellar spider, and the harvestman.

Deer generally don't live in forests. They prefer open or semi-open terrain.

You can not tell the age of a male **deer** by the number of points on its antlers. Their antlers grow each year, but the number of points is dependent on genetic makeup and recent health.

Diamondback rattlers do not necessarily rattle before attacking. They often strike without warning. In fact, they're deaf so they don't even know when they are rattling.

The old saying "You can't teach an old **dog** new tricks" is not true. Older dogs are just as capable of learning tricks as younger dogs.

Multiplying a **dog**'s age by seven doesn't provide an accurate equivalent to the age of a human. Dogs mature very rapidly—they are closer to the human equivalent of fifteen after their first year. Plus, dogs age at different rates depending on their size, e.g., smaller dogs usually live longer.

A **dog's** mouth is not cleaner than a human's. While most of the bacteria in a dog's mouth are not dangerous to humans, just remember some of the interesting objects they've licked or put in their mouths, e.g., dead animals.

Dogs don't sweat through their tongue. Their sweat glands are in their paws. They keep themselves cool, however, by panting and cooling off their tongue.

Dogs aren't color blind. Their ability to see color is not as good as humans, but they definitely recognize several different colors.

There's no difference between **doves and pigeons**—they are all members of the columbidae family. "Dove" comes from Old English, while "Pigeon" comes from a French word. Bird experts do tend to label smaller species as "doves," and larger species as "pigeons." And colloquially, most folks think of the white ones as doves and the gray ones in the park as pigeons. But they really are all in the same family.

There's no truth to the claim a **duck**'s quack doesn't echo. Any sound can echo.

A **duck** does not need to bob its head to walk. Ducks are often seen walking without moving their head.

An **earthworm** cannot survive as two living worms when cut in two. At most, only one half will survive.

Earwigs don't crawl into ears. They're called that because their hind legs appear to be ear-shaped.

Electric eels are not eels. They are freshwater fish related to the carp.

There is no such thing as an **elephant** graveyard where elephants go to die. Elephant bodies disappear quickly in the jungle because of scavengers, decay, and rapid growth of vegetation.

Elephants aren't afraid of mice. In fact, it is unlikely an elephant, given its poor eyesight, would even know a mouse was nearby.

Elephants don't drink water through their trunks. They pick up water with their trunks and put it in their mouths.

A **firefly** is not a fly. It's a type of beetle.

There is no leader in a school of **fish**. The group movements of a school of fish may appear simultaneous, but they can be started by any fish in the group. Fish react very quickly to the movement of the fish nearest to them, so the school only appears to follow a single leader.

Flying fish don't fly. They propel themselves out of the water and glide.

Flying squirrels don't fly. They just jump and glide exceptionally well.

French poodles did not originate in France. They were originally bred in Germany.

The first animal sent into space was not a monkey or a dog. It was a **fruit fly**.

Giraffes do not have more vertebrae in their neck than other animals. They have the same number and they're just farther apart.

Goats don't eat tin cans. They may nibble on them like anything else in their way, but they will not actually swallow one.

Goldfish don't have a memory of only three seconds. Scientists have trained goldfish to navigate mazes, with the memory staying up to three months.

Gorillas are not aggressive towards humans in their natural habitat. They are gentle and shy, and only attack if provoked.

The **gray whale** is not gray. It's black.

The **Great Dane** dog did not originate in Denmark. It originated in Germany.

The "grey" in **greyhound** does not refer to the dog's color. It's from an Old Norse term meaning "bitch."

Grizzly bears were not named because they are "grisly" killers. "Grizzly" means "gray-haired." Though they appear to be mostly brown, their fur is generally silver-tipped.

Guinea pigs did not originate in Guinea and are not pigs. They are rodents from South America.

Though their name is often associated with a scientific test participant, **guinea pigs** are rarely used as subjects in experiments. Mice, rats, and rabbits are much more common.

The most common use for **guinea pigs** is not as a test subject or as a family pet. The vast majority are eaten in South American countries.

Hens don't sit on their eggs. They squat with their weight mostly on their legs so they don't crush the egg.

The African mammal that kills the most humans is not the lion. It's the **hippopotamus**.

Homing pigeons aren't born with a natural ability to find their way home from a long distance. Their return visits are only possible through careful, time-consuming training, e.g., gradually increasing the distance they learn to fly home.

Horns and antlers are not the same thing. Horns are part of the animal's skull and are attached for life. Antlers are not part of the skull and drop off each year.

Horned toads are not toads. They are lizards.

Hornets are no more dangerous than bees and wasps. In fact, they are not as aggressive and rarely sting. Their sting is only life-threatening if their victim is allergic to the hornet's poison.

Not all **horses** sleep standing up. They will sleep standing up if there's not enough room, but they will likely sleep lying down if given the opportunity.

Horseshoe crabs are not crabs, or any sort of crustacean. They're the only survivors of an entirely different species that nearly became extinct 175 million years ago.

Hummingbirds don't hum. The sound you hear is the beating of their wings.

Jellyfish aren't fish. They are cnidaria. Other than living in the sea, jellyfish and fish have little in common, e.g., jellyfish have no vertebrae, while all fish are vertebrates.

Kangaroos didn't get their name when Captain Cook asked aborigines what they were, and they replied in their native tongue, "I don't understand." The word for this creature in the aborigine language is the very similar "gangurru."

The sting of African **killer bees** is no more lethal than that of U.S. honey bees. They are more aggressive and tend to protect a very large area around their hive, but their sting is similar.

Killer whales, or, more accurately, orcas, are not whales. They are a type of dolphin.

The **kiwi bird** was not named after the kiwi fruit. The fruit, aka the Chinese gooseberry, was named for the bird.

Koalas are not bears. They are marsupials.

Though **Koalas** are peaceful and lethargic during the daytime, they aren't like that 24 hours a day. At nighttime, they are active and even dangerous if disturbed.

The **Komodo dragon** is not a dragon. It's a lizard.

Labrador retrievers did not originate in Labrador. They originated in Newfoundland.

Ladybugs aren't all females. Because they appear about the same time as the Catholic celebration of Annunciation, they were named after the Virgin Mary.

Herds of **lemmings** don't throw themselves in the sea. The suicide run of lemmings is fictitious, staged by the Disney Company in a documentary called "White Wilderness."

While movie character Napoleon Dynamite's silly description would suggest otherwise, **ligers** are not fictitious. Bred in captivity, they are the offspring of a male lion and a female tiger. The offspring of a male tiger and a female lion is a tigon.

Most **mammals** are not monogamous. In fact, only 3% are monogamous.

Monkeys aren't looking for insects when they pick at the skin of other monkeys. They're looking for salty bits of loose skin—apparently a big treat in monkey land.

Monkeys aren't always perfectly agile when swinging from tree to tree. Experts estimate several thousand monkeys die each year from falling.

The deadliest animal on Earth is not the shark, bear, lion, or any of the animals we consider ferocious. The animal responsible for the most deaths is, by far, the **mosquito**.

Those red bumps you get in the summer aren't literally **mosquito** bites. Mosquitoes don't bite. They stab your skin with a sharp proboscis and then suck blood out.

Adjusting your diet does not deter **mosquitoes**. For example, they are just as likely to seek your blood even if you have eaten garlic.

Moths are not attracted to light. Moths use light rays from the sun and the moon for navigation, so their flight path gets jumbled when there's another source of light nearby.

Mules are not the same as donkeys. They are the offspring of a male donkey and a female horse.

Opossums don't hang from their tails, and baby opossums don't hang off their mothers' tails. They sometimes grab a tree branch with their tail for balance, but they aren't able to support their weight with their tail.

Opossums don't "play possum," i.e., pretend to be dead. They usually hiss and snap when cornered. They sometimes remain still, but that's because they go into a catatonic state of fear.

Ostriches don't bury their heads in the sand. The common belief is they do this to hide from their enemies. In fact, they have plenty of speed if they want to elude attackers.

Panthers are not a species. Panther is a generic name for any big cat (leopards, jaguars, or cougars) with a black coat.

No **penguins** live in the Arctic. But, then again, not all **penguins** live on Antarctica. Several types of penguins are found in the southern parts of Africa, Australia, New Zealand, and South America. Some even thrive in relatively warm climates.

Pigs rarely overeat, and are certainly less likely to overeat than humans.

Pink flamingos aren't really pink. They are born gray and gain color based on what they eat, e.g., shrimp. White flamingos aren't a different genus—they just have different diets.

Piranhas aren't nearly as deadly as most people think. There are no known human deaths from a piranha attack. In fact, even non-lethal bites from piranhas are rare..

The fur on **polar bears** is not white. The individual hairs are transparent. The effect, however, is that the fur appears white.

Pony is not a name for a young horse. The correct name is foal. The term pony describes several breeds of horses that are small, and does not relate to the age of the horse.

No **ponies** were ever used in the Pony Express. They were horses—ponies don't have the strength for rapid, long-distance riding.

Porcupines cannot shoot their quills at an aggressor. The quills are only dislodged when the aggressor comes in contact with the porcupine.

The **prairie dog** is not a dog. It's a rodent.

A female **praying mantis** does not typically kill and eat its partner after having sex. This does occur in captivity, but a praying mantis only rarely does this in the wild.

A **purple finch** isn't purple. It's crimson.

The **quarter horse** was not given that name because of its size. They are called that because they excelled at race distances of a quarter mile.

Rabbits and **hares** are not the same thing. Hares tend to be larger, have longer ears and legs, and live more in isolation than rabbits.

Rats are not, by definition, dirty and diseased. Wild rats are effective scavengers that can survive in conditions humans don't find particularly appealing, but rats kept as pets are actually very clean. In fact, they regularly wash themselves and clean up their living environment.

There is no fish called **red herring**. The herring only turns red after it is smoked and salted.

Though the giant panda is a bear, the smaller **red panda** is not. It's related to the raccoon.

The first domesticated animal was not a dog, a cat, or a horse. It was a **reindeer**—domesticated in Russia long ago.

Reindeer are not deer. They belong to the caribou family.

There is no fish called a **sardine**. Those small fish in a tin can are usually herring.

The **screech owl** doesn't screech. Its only sound is a soft wail.

Sea cucumbers are not cucumbers, or any sort of plant. Like starfish, they are echinoderms.

Not all **sharks** are dangerous to humans. About eighty percent of shark species are incapable of harming humans.

Sharks don't have poor eyesight. They can see remarkably well in very dim light. They use other senses to search for prey, but they also use their very powerful eyes.

There are no **Siberian tigers** in Siberia. While some tigers in this endangered group still survive in southeastern Russia, none live in Siberia.

A **silkworm** is not a worm. It's a caterpillar.

The two-toed **sloth** doesn't have just two toes. It has three on each foot, or six altogether. They do, however, have only two fingers on each of their hands.

Forcing a **spider** down the drain with flowing water doesn't always kill it. Spiders are very buoyant and can usually float back to the surface.

People do not swallow, on average, eight **spiders** a year. This statistic was a hoax used in a computing magazine to show how quickly rumors spread across the Internet.

Squirrels can't remember where they hid acorns and other nuts. They are able to find them because they have a great sense of smell.

Starfish aren't fish. They're echinoderms, a class of animal with several distinct differences from fish, e.g., they have no backbone.

No known **St. Bernard** has ever carried a small brandy barrel around its neck. Their rescue missions in mountain areas have always been alcohol-free.

Swallows don't return to California's San Juan Capistrano Mission on the same date every year. The common belief is they always return on March 19, St. Joseph's Day. In fact, they can arrive on any date from late February to late March.

Swans don't sing a beautiful song, i.e., a "swan song," as they die. They may make various noises, such as croaks and hisses—the same noises they make throughout their life.

Tarantulas are not dangerous. They only bite if provoked, and their bite is relatively harmless.

Thoroughbred is not the name used for horses to indicate they have a pedigree. Like other animals, purebred is the correct term. A thoroughbred is a specific breed of horse bred for racing.

India does not have the highest population of **tigers**. That distinction now goes to the United States. There are more tigers in captivity in the U.S. than the number still surviving in India.

The **titmouse** is not a mouse. It's a bird.

Animals aren't more common in rural areas. In fact, more species tend to be found in urban areas. **Urban climates** are generally milder and excess food, e.g., trash, is plentiful.

A **velvet ant** is not an ant. It's a wasp.

Whales do not blow water through their blow holes. They exhale warm air, which becomes vapor when it comes in contact with the cold air over the water. The vapor only looks like water.

Wild dogs howl, whine, growl, and yelp, but they don't bark. Barking is limited to domesticated dogs. One theory is that barking is an attempt at a human-like sound.

The use of the term **wolf** to describe a womanizer is unfair. Male wolves are monogamous for life and share parenting duties with the female.

Wolves are not ferocious and do not attack humans. They're very docile and often friendlier than many dogs.

Wolves don't howl at the moon. They arch their back when they howl, appearing to look at the moon, but are actually communicating with others in their pack.

There is not one single authenticated case of a pack of **wolves** raising a human child. The only thing odder than these strange stories is the fact these stories are commonly believed.

Art

Not all paintings considered part of the **cubism** movement depict cubical shapes. Cones, cylinders, and spheres are also very common.

Leonardo da Vinci's famous painting in the Louvre is not called the "Mona Lisa." Its official title is "La Gioconda."

It's not true most great painters become famous after their **death**. While Van Gogh was fairly unknown during his lifetime, most master painters, e.g., Michelangelo, da Vinci, Picasso, were highly regarded and in high demand.

Walt Disney did not draw Mickey Mouse. The original artist was Walt's assistant, Ub Iwerks. However, Walt was the original voice of Mickey.

The great painter **El Greco** was not Spanish. His popular name was just a nickname describing his nationality, Greek. He was born Domenikos Theotokopoulos.

Classic **Greek sculptures** were not all white. Many were originally painted with bright colors, but now only survive with the original base color of white.

Unlike the persona depicted in movies, **Michelangelo** was not a moody loner who could not work with others. He was, in fact, an entrepreneur of a small business, generally hiring 10-20 assistants to help complete projects he had negotiated with sponsors.

Pablo Picasso didn't always paint abstract art. He painted professionally for almost ten years before he became interested in cubism.

Rembrandt's "The Night Watch" was not a huge failure that led to his downfall and near bankruptcy. The painting was not criticized during his lifetime. His money problems were largely a result of his extravagant tastes.

Norman Rockwell wasn't the only cover artist for "The Saturday Evening Post." He painted less than a third of the magazine's covers.

The misconception exists because most Saturday Evening Post cover artists used a style generally associated with Rockwell.

Auguste Rodin's bronze statue of a man sitting with his chin on his hand is not called "The Thinker." Its actual name is "The Poet."

Painter **Vincent Van Gogh** did not cut off his entire ear. He only cut off a small portion of the ear lobe.

James Whistler's famous painting of his mother was never titled "Whistler's Mother." Whistler originally named it "Arrangement in Gray and Black." Later, Whistler renamed it "Portrait of My Mother."

Aviation

Airplane tires do not wear out from the impact of landings. They endure more wear while taxiing on the tarmac. The severe turns around the tarmac cause considerable lateral wear on the tires.

There is no such thing as an **air pocket**. You feel turbulence when your plane encounters either a downdraft or updraft.

Large airplanes are not designed to withstand all collisions with **birds**. They are only designed to withstand collisions with birds weighing four pounds or less. Many birds weigh over four pounds, and, in fact, there are approximately 3,000 airplane collisions with large birds each year. Some collisions can be dangerous—at least five major airplane accidents have been at least partially attributed to a collision with a bird.

Planes never intentionally dump **blue ice** toilet waste while in flight. They store toilet water until they land. Instances where blue ice fell from the sky were due to accidental leakages.

The **black box** in airplanes is not black. It's bright orange.

Despite what you've seen in several movies, humans aren't necessarily sucked out of a plane when the passenger compartment is suddenly **depressurized**, e.g., a window is shot out. Planes are not completely airtight, so the pressure difference between the inside and outside is not that significant. In fact, passengers without seat belts have remained in their seats after the fuselage roof was torn open.

Amelia Earhart did not disappear while flying alone around the world. She had a navigator with her during the flight.

Dressing nice doesn't increase your chances of upgrading to **first class**. In fact, nothing besides participation in a frequent flying program, or cold hard cash, will enable you to be upgraded. Airlines might have done favors for passengers in the past, but not anymore.

United States **Interstate Highways** were never designed as possible airplane landings. Supposedly, a straight and flat stretch must occur every ten miles. The legend is probably based on the German Autobahn, where such planning did take place.

Charles Lindberg wasn't the first to cross the Atlantic in a plane. He was the first to do it flying solo.

Most or all passengers do not die in **plane crashes**. Only 4.3% of plane crash passengers die.

Being in the tail is not the most dangerous place in a **plane crash**. Those sitting in the tail section have a 40% greater chance of surviving than the other passengers, including those seated near the exits.

Breathing **recycled air** in commercial planes does not increase your chances of getting sick. There are excellent filters on airplanes that extract virtually all of the potential germs and viruses from the air. It may even be cleaner than the air you breathe on the ground.

The **Spruce Goose**, the huge wooden plane made by Howard Hughes in the 1940s, was not made of spruce. It was made of birch.

The **Wright brothers**' airplane was not called the "Kitty Hawk." That's the name of the town where the 1903 flight took place. The plane was called the "Wright Flyer."

Business

In all likelihood, the **Baby Ruth candy bar** was not named for Babe Ruth or President Grover Cleveland's daughter, Ruth. It was probably named for the granddaughter of the company's owner.

There was no such person as **Betty Crocker**. She was fabricated by the General Mills Food Company to increase sales. The name was a tribute to General Mills' CEO, William G. Crocker.

Coca-Cola did not create New Coke as a marketing ploy to increase the sale of Classic Coke. They intended to sell New Coke exclusively.

In terms of sales, the **Friday after Thanksgiving** is not the busiest shopping day of the year. More purchases are made on the Saturday before Christmas.

Charles Wilson, former President of **General Motors**, never said, "What's good for General Motors is good for the country." He said, "For years I thought what was good for our country was good for General Motors—and vice versa."

The **Heinz Company** does not have, and has never had, exactly 57 varieties. That number was picked out of thin air.

Lloyd's of London is not an insurance company. It's a society of many separate insurance companies housed in the same location.

The **Quaker Oats Company** was not formed by Quakers or run by Quakers. Its only connection is that the company originated in Pennsylvania, where many American Quakers are located.

Colonel Sanders, the founder and now symbol of Kentucky Fried Chicken, was not an actual military colonel. He was given the honorary title of colonel by the governor of Kentucky.

When visiting **Sea World**, you're not seeing the famous orca named Shamu. You're seeing one of many orcas named Shamu. All four Sea World parks name their performing orca Shamu.

Subliminal messages don't work. No marketing study has shown a sales increase after the use of subliminal messages.

The famous **Walt Disney** signature used in the company logo is not really his signature. It was designed by a company artist.

Though the name **Wells Fargo** is associated with stagecoaches in the old West, owners Henry Wells and William Fargo rarely left New York City. In fact, Fargo never once left New York.

The **Wienerschnitzel** fast food franchise offers lots of hot dogs, but no wiener schnitzel. A wiener schnitzel is a veal patty fried in a coating of bread crumbs, and probably not what most fast food customers are looking for.

Consumer Products

The name of the sports apparel company, **Adidas**, is not an acronym for "All Day I Dream about Sports" or "All Day I Dream about Sex." The company's founder is Adolph "Adi" Dassler. Adidas is a combination of his nickname and the first three letters of his last name.

Aerosol and liquid **air fresheners** do not remove bad odors from the air. They produce a stronger odor that overpowers the bad odor.

Neither the shiny side nor the less shiny side of **aluminum foil** is better for cooking or storing. They're the same and only look different because of the way it's manufactured.

Despite scientific-sounding emails, **antiperspirants** do not cause breast cancer. Research has shown this is a myth.

Bottles of **aspirin** don't contain cotton to ensure freshness. The wads of cotton are there to prevent the aspirin tablets from breaking if the bottle is dropped.

Banana oil is not derived from bananas. It is petroleum oil with a scent somewhat similar to a banana.

The **Barbie doll** did not originate in the United States. The Mattel Company found her in Germany, where the doll was sold as a gag for stag parties.

Storing **batteries** in a refrigerator or a freezer does not improve their performance. In fact, battery manufacturers recommend storing batteries at room temperature.

Blackboards are no longer typically black. They are more likely to be green.

The original **boomerangs** were not designed to return to the thrower. They were used in war and hunting to kill a target from a distance. Generally, only those used for sport are designed to return.

Camel's hair brushes contain no camel's hair. Hair from squirrels' tails is usually used. A cute, but unsubstantiated story is that a fellow named Mr. Camel marketed these brushes.

Using a **cell phone** at a gas station is not particularly dangerous. There are no documented cases of a cell phone spark starting a gas station fire.

Cell phones don't cause brain cancer. Those studies that have been well designed and look at a large population have found no connection.

You don't use **chalk** on a blackboard. That white stuff is calcined gypsum, which is the same thing as plaster of Paris.

Chamois does not come from the Alpine goat-like animal with the same name. It's usually sheepskin.

Diamonds are not the most valuable gem. Rubies usually sell for about four times the cost of diamonds.

Not all **diamonds** are clear and colorless. The more expensive ones used in jewelry are colorless, but most diamonds have color. These diamonds are frequently used in industry for drilling or cutting.

Diamond rings were not frequently given as engagement rings until the 1930s. The custom only became popular after a diamond company worked with Hollywood to glamorize the idea of diamond engagement rings.

Dry cleaning is not dry. The clothes are immersed in a liquid. They are just not exposed to water.

Electric fans do not cool the room. You feel cooler in a room with a fan because the fan blows the warm air radiated by your body away from your skin. If you're sweaty, they also help by turning the moisture on your skin into vapor. So fans are useful, but you're wasting electricity if you turn them on to cool an empty room.

India ink is not from India. It's from China.

Clothing **irons** are no longer made of iron. The "sole plate" of this appliance is made of aluminum or stainless steel.

Lead crystal is not a crystal. It's a type of glass.

Lead pencils have no lead. That's graphite in them.

Low nicotine cigarettes don't reduce the negative effects of tobacco. People who smoke low nicotine cigarettes are just as addicted to nicotine as those who smoke cigarettes with a regular amount of nicotine. Smokers using the low nicotine version tend to suck harder and more often to accommodate their addiction.

Those **mattress and pillow tags** that say "Under penalty of law, this tag is not to be removed" do not apply to you. In fact, the warning also says "Except by consumer." They only apply to the folks who sell the mattresses and pillows. The warnings are designed to protect consumers.

Microwave ovens don't cause cancer. They give off less radiation than a rock. In fact, X-rays aside, the number one source for radiation in your life is the ground below you.

Microwave ovens don't cook the middle part of food first. In fact, just the opposite is true—microwaves cook food from the outside in. Consumers are fooled because Hot Pockets and other products often have a scalding hot center. This is because foods with high water content cook faster in a microwave. The cheese in the center cooks faster than the low-water crust.

Not all metals arc and cause damage when placed in a **microwave**. Electric arcing depends on the shape and size of the metal, and the length of time it's in the microwave. Certain metal products, such as browning sleeves and pizza platforms, do not arc.

Panama hats did not originate in Panama. They originated in Ecuador.

There's no advantage to choosing **paper bags** over plastic bags at the supermarket. They require considerably more energy to manufacture, create more air and water pollution, and, because of weight, cost more to transport. Neither paper nor plastic is a better choice.

31

It is no better to use a **plastic cutting board** than a wood one. In fact, scientific tests show bacteria die much quicker on wood compared to plastic.

Portland cement does not come from Portland, Oregon or Portland, Maine. It's called that because it resembles stone found on the Isle of Portland in England.

Rice paper is not made from rice. It's from a Taiwanese tree called Tetrapanax papyrifer.

A hot water or steam **radiator** does not radiate heat. It transfers energy by convection.

Higher SPF numbers on **sunscreens** do not necessarily indicate greater protection. There is no discernable extra protection as SPF numbers increase beyond 30. In fact, the FDA wants to limit sunscreens at 30 so folks don't have the false impression they can stay out longer when they use higher SPF sunscreens.

While it's true the **teddy bear** was named for President Teddy Roosevelt, the bear did not originate in the United States. The Steiff Company in Germany created the first teddy bears.

A **ten-gallon hat** doesn't hold ten gallons. It would probably hold about ¾ of a gallon.

That stuff you use to wrap your leftovers is not **tin foil**. It's now exclusively made with aluminum.

A **two-by-four** is not two inches by four inches. It's 1 ¾ inches by 3 ½ inches.

Venetian blinds did not originate in Venice. They originated in Japan.

Zinc supplements do not get rid of white spots on your fingernails. Those white spots are caused by minor damage to the nail. Only new growth in the nail will make the spots disappear.

Drugs and Alcohol

Drinking **alcohol** does not warm you up on a cold day. You may momentarily feel warmer, but alcohol actually decreases your body temperature.

Though it can make some people very silly, **alcohol** is not a stimulant. It's a depressant. It also depresses the inhibitory center of the brain, which leads to loss of inhabitation and behavior easily confused with stimulation.

Not all **alcohol** evaporates during cooking. For example, about 85 percent of the alcohol remains in a quickly cooked flambé. It would take at least three hours of cooking to burn off all the alcohol in most dishes.

It's not possible to create a hallucinogenic drug from **bananas**. The rumor that banana peels can provide an LSD-like effect grew after folks misinterpreted Donovan's song "Mellow Yellow."

Placing a penny under your tongue will not help you pass a **Breathalyzer** test. This is a silly hoax spread via the Internet.

Cocaine does not make sex better. In fact, long-term use typically results in reduced sex drive and even impotence.

Drinking **coffee** does not sober you up any quicker. Your body processes alcohol at a constant rate, so nothing you ingest will speed up the process.

Ecstasy does not put holes in the brain or cause Parkinson's disease. The jury is still out on the amount of brain damage Ecstasy may or may not cause, but there is no evidence either of these two effects has ever occurred.

Most **fatal drug overdoses** are not the result of illegal drugs. Deaths from prescription drugs overdoses outnumber all of the illegal drugs combined.

The "cotton fever" some users get from shooting **heroin** is not from the use of cotton when injecting. Because cotton is used as a filter when shooting up, some users believe the cotton particles could cause a nasty fever. In truth, the fever was from endocarditis, caused by the use of non-sterile equipment.

Taking **ibuprofen** does not cause false positives for marijuana on drug tests. This was previously true, but blood tests have been corrected.

A **Long Island Iced Tea** has no tea. It does, however, have vodka, gin, tequila, and rum.

No evidence exists that "blue star tattoos" laced with **LSD** were ever distributed to school children. Supposedly, dealers put LSD on lick-and-stick tattoos depicting a blue star, and passed them out to children in hopes of creating an addiction and an ongoing revenue stream. Not only there is no evidence this ever happened, but it doesn't make sense—LSD is not addictive.

There is likely no such thing as "bad acid," or **LSD** that has somehow been contaminated and therefore creates a "bad trip." Doses are generally too small to introduce any sort of dangerous containment. "Bad trips" are likely the result of overly high doses of LSD.

No known individuals went blind while staring at the sun during an **LSD** trip. The myth became popular after it appeared on a 1967 episode of Dragnet.

Marijuana is not 10-20 times more potent than it was in the 60s and 70s. It appears that potency has risen only about 3 times as much.

Tobacco companies have not placed patents on certain strains of **marijuana** in anticipation of its eventual legalization. Philip Morris supposedly patented "Marlboro Greens," but there is no evidence this ever occurred.

There is no evidence **marijuana** is a gateway drug. A Rand Corporation study, among others, debunked that myth. In fact, in countries where marijuana has been legalized, it appears marijuana usage often replaces hard drug usage, and results in fewer emergency room visits.

Inhaling crystal **methamphetamine** smoke does not cause lung damage. The byproduct is highly water soluble and is instantly absorbed into the blood stream. The myth probably surfaced because Ritalin administered with an IV has caused lung damage. The culprit was the talc from Ritalin tablets that were crushed for the IV solution.

Psychedelic **mushrooms** are not common mushrooms laced with a hallucinogenic, such as LSD. Psilocybin mushrooms naturally produce hallucinogenic effects. That said, some shady dealers have been known to sell regular mushrooms laced with LSD to save a few bucks.

Taking high doses of **Niacin** does not help you pass a drug test. Supposedly, Niacin burns drugs out of your system, but there's no truth to this claim.

PCP is not embalming fluid, i.e., formaldehyde, or even related to it. It is sometimes nicknamed "embalming fluid" because it creates a strong feeling of dissociation.

The "33" shown on bottles of **Rolling Rock beer** does not stand for the year Prohibition ended. It was a word count at the bottom of the label that snuck by the printers. It gained popularity and is now closely associated with the product.

Sloe gin is not a type of gin. It's a liqueur.

Whiskey did not originate in Scotland. It was first created in China.

The color of **wine** is not determined by the color of the grapes. White wine is made with grapes fermented without their skins. Red wine is from grapes fermented with their skins.

Using corks, rather than screw top metal caps, is no better for bottled **wine**. Because fancier wines are usually bottled with a cork, there's a misconception corks are better at preserving the flavor. In fact, mold can form in cork, and leaves the wine flat and musty tasting. Screw top caps are considerably less likely to taint the flavor of the wine.

The Earth

It doesn't snow much in **Antarctica**. The annual snowfall is about an inch. It just looks like a lot of snow because so little of it melts.

The **Arctic** is not a continent or an island. It is ice cover over a large ocean.

Even though all 50 of the world's tallest mountains are there, **Asia** is not the highest continent. The continent with the highest average elevation is Antarctica.

Avalanches are not typically caused by loud noises. The more frequent cause is someone stepping or skiing across a weak spot in a large bank of snow.

The **Bermuda Triangle** is no more dangerous than any other 400,000 square mile body of water. A study by Lloyd's of London found traveling through this very large area presented no greater risk than any other similarly sized area.

If you dug straight through the Earth from the United States, you wouldn't end up in **China**. You would end up in the middle of the Indian Ocean, west of Australia.

A **cyclone** is not a weather phenomenon distinct from tornadoes and hurricanes. A cyclone is any pattern of circulating winds in a low pressure area. Tornadoes and hurricanes are, therefore, types of cyclones.

Death Valley in California is not the hottest place on Earth. El Azizia in Libya had the highest recorded temperature—136 degrees.

Deserts are not always hot, sandy places. Any region that has very little precipitation, and is largely uninhabitable, is considered a desert. In fact, the interior of Antarctica is a desert.

Contrary to the term "dewfall," **dew** does not fall from the sky. Water droplets form on your lawn when moisture from the air condenses faster than it can evaporate.

The **Earth** is not round. It's close to round, but it's slightly flat at each of the poles.

It's not safe to leave shelter during the **eye of a hurricane**. While the storm tends to be relatively calm in the center, it is still dangerously close to high winds that can appear without warning.

Glaciers aren't only found near the North and South Poles. There is a glacier on the equator—Mt. Cotopaxi in Ecuador.

The **humidity** described by weather reporters is not the actual percentage of moisture in the air. That's the absolute humidity, and is usually less than 5%. The weather folks report the relative humidity, which is the current absolute humidity divided by the area's maximum absolute humidity. A 90% relative humidity means it's close to an area's worst possible humidity—not that the air is 90% full of moisture.

There's no rule that says **hurricane** names can only be used once. While the names of particularly famous hurricanes, e.g., Katrina, will probably never be used again, lesser known hurricane names can be reused.

Leaving your windows open during a **hurricane** does not reduce damage to your home. Supposedly, this reduces air pressure build-up and prevents significant destruction. It's better to close the windows and keep all that wind and debris out of your house.

The most recent **ice age** never ended. We're still in it. Geographers define an ice age as any period when there are at least polar ice caps. Until those disappear, we're still in an ice age.

Icebergs are not frozen ocean water. They are pieces of ice that have broken off from glaciers or ice sheets.

Lightning does not occur before thunder. They are part of the same event and occur at the same time. Light travels faster than sound, so you see it before you hear it.

It's not true **lightning** doesn't strike twice in the same spot. If lightning made it to a certain spot once, there's a reasonable chance the same weather conditions will arise and there will be a recurrence. Lighting strikes the Empire State Building about 100 times a year.

Lightning bolts don't travel towards the ground. They travel upwards to the sky.

Being inside does not provide sure-proof safety from a **lightning storm**. In fact, more lightning-related deaths occur indoors than outdoors. The numbers are skewed by the fact that most people go indoors during a lightning storm, but proximity to various indoor electrical objects (e.g., appliances) has resulted in many deaths. That said, it's still safer indoors than outdoors.

The **Mayan Calendar** never predicted the world would come to an end on December 21, 2012. It's simply the date the calendar rolls over to day zero and starts over again. Nothing in Mayan writings or legend suggested the world would end on this date.

The air we breathe is not all **oxygen**, or even mostly oxygen. It's 80 percent nitrogen.

The most common material in the world is not water. It's **perovskite**, the material that makes up the earth's mantle. Though no one has ever taken a sample of it, scientists have determined it's a mineral compound of magnesium, silicon, and oxygen.

Though it seems to fall fast, **rain** only travels about 7 mph. Drizzling rain only falls about 1-2 mph.

The primary tool used by seismologists to measure earthquakes is not the **Richter scale**. It's the MMS, or Moment Magnitude Scale. It was created to better measure the total impact of the quake.

Riptides aren't tides. They're currents.

Seasons are not the result of the Earth being closer or farther from the sun at different times of the year. They result from how the Earth tilts over the course of a year, i.e., the Northern Hemisphere tilts closest to the sun at the beginning of summer.

The **sky** is not blue because that's the color of space, or because it's reflecting off the ocean. It's blue because the blue wavelengths of the sun are absorbed and then radiated by gasses in the atmosphere.

Big, dangerous waves are not **tidal waves**. They are tsunamis. The tide has little to do with the size of these waves.

Toilet water does not drain counterclockwise in toilets in the northern hemisphere in the same way ocean currents travel counterclockwise north of the equator. If the toilet water does drain that direction, it's because of the design of the toilet, e.g., placement of jets.

Water is not completely colorless. It has a blue tinge. It's very faint and can only be seen in large bodies of water, but it's there.

The **winter solstice** in the Northern hemisphere does not always fall on December 21. Though it always falls on that date in leap years, it is more likely to fall on December 22 in non-leap years.

Famous People

Johnny Appleseed was not a fictional character. Born John Chapman, Mr. Appleseed wandered through the Midwest for many years, planting apples as a symbolic theme in his missionary work for his church.

Though the National Audubon Society is dedicated to the conservation of wildlife, **John J. Audubon** was not a preservationist. He was an avid hunter who was very talented at drawing detailed pictures of birds.

P.T. Barnum didn't say, "There's a sucker born every minute." There's no evidence he ever said it, and his biographer insists it would be very uncharacteristic of him to say it.

Clara Barton was not the founder of the Red Cross. She created the American Red Cross in 1882. Swiss banker Jean-Henri Dunant created the International Red Cross in 1864.

Billy the Kid's real name was not William H. Bonney. That was just the alias he was using when he was sentenced to death. He was born Henry McCarty.

Napoleon Bonaparte wasn't short. He was average height, but remembered as short because a mistake was made at his autopsy.

Lizzie Borden was never found guilty of ax murdering her parents. In fact, the jury only took an hour of deliberation to acquit her of all charges.

It's not true President **George H.W. Bush** had never heard of a supermarket scanner when it was demonstrated to him at a 1988 grocers' convention. While he was inquisitive and enthusiastic as exhibitors described the potential of the devices, he was already familiar with supermarket scanners.

Julius Caesar was probably not born by cesarean section. The surgical techniques used at the time would have left his mother dead. The term "cesarean" just sounds like "Caesar." It is actually derived from the Latin term for "cut."

Russian empress **Catherine the Great** did not die while having sex with a horse, nor is there evidence she had any encounters with the equine community. She died from a stroke while sitting on the toilet.

Winston Churchill didn't create the term "iron curtain." It originated many years before Churchill made it famous.

Cleopatra was not an Egyptian. She was from the Ptolemaic dynasty of rulers from Macedonia, and spoke Greek.

The fellow who hijacked a plane and parachuted with cash into a Pacific Northwest forest in 1971 was never identified by officials as **D.B. Cooper**. The FBI searched for Dan Cooper, the name the hijacker used when checking on the flight. One suspect for a short time was a fellow named D.B. Cooper, but he was ruled out when it was learned he was in prison at the time.

Copernicus was not the first person to claim the Earth travels around the sun. An ancient mathematician named Aristarchus suggested this over 1800 years earlier.

Contrary to the John Wayne movie, **Davy Crockett** didn't blow up the ammunition supply as he was stabbed to death defending the Alamo. Crockett surrendered, and was then executed by a firing squad.

Charles Darwin was not the first to describe evolution theory. Ancient Greeks and various philosophers had discussed the idea centuries before Darwin published his classic, On the Origin of Species. Darwin's greatest contribution was the collection of data that supported the theory.

Charles Darwin did not coin the phrase "Survival of the Fittest." The credit should go to Herbert Spencer.

Walt Disney's body was not cryogenically stored. He was cremated in Glendale, California.

Albert Einstein was not awarded the Nobel Prize for his work on the Theory of Relativity. It was considered controversial at the time, so the Nobel folks awarded Einstein the prize for his lesser known work on the photoelectric effect of light.

Albert Einstein was not a poor student in school. Records show Einstein was "brilliant" in school, e.g., he was conversant in college-level physics at the age of 11.

Ralph Waldo Emerson did not say, "Consistency is the hobgoblin of little minds." He said "A foolish consistency is the hobgoblin of little minds." The correct quote only criticizes "foolish consistency," not consistency in general.

Despite his reputation as the "father of geometry," **Euclid** did not "invent" geometry. Most of the major concepts were established before Euclid's time. His great contribution was that he compiled all of the concepts and put them in a series of thirteen books, called <u>Elements</u>.

Benjamin Franklin did not discover electricity. The concept was well understood when he flew a kite in a storm. And his kite was not struck by lightning; otherwise, he would have been killed. He demonstrated that a small electrical charge could be obtained from a storm cloud, implying that lightning was electrical in nature.

Robert Fulton's first steamboat was not called the Clermont. It was named the North River Steamboat. It was later renamed for Clermont, one of the ports Fulton's boat stopped at.

Vice President **Al Gore** never said he "invented the Internet." He was describing legislation he supported to make the Internet possible.

Contrary to the punch line of the silly joke, **Ulysses S. Grant** was not buried in Grant's Tomb. You're only buried if your body is put under ground. Grant's body was "entombed" above the ground.

John Hancock did not use an especially large signature on the Declaration of Independence to show extra defiance towards the British. He generally used a large and flamboyant signature, plus, being the first to sign, he had lots of space to work with.

Sir Edmund Hillary, one of the first climbers to reach the summit of Mt. Everest, didn't say, "Because it's there," when asked why he wanted to climb the mountain. It was said by George Mallory, who died on the mountain nearly 30 years earlier.

Magician **Harry Houdini** didn't die as he performed one of his magic tricks, e.g., the Hollywood biopic has him escaping from a water torture cell. He died from a ruptured appendix after he challenged a medical student to hit him in the stomach.

Though he wasn't the nicest man in history, **Ivan the Terrible** did not receive his nickname because he was considered evil. He was probably no more evil than most rulers of his day. A better translation of the Russian word "grozny," Ivan's nickname, is "formidable."

Railroad engineer **Casey Jones** wasn't a fictional character in a children's story. He was an actual engineer who died on a foggy day in 1900 when his speeding train crashed into the rear of a freight train.

Revolutionary War hero **John Paul Jones** was not a particularly heroic, or even honorable, sea captain before the American Navy assigned a ship to him. He began his career as a slave ship captain and changed his name after the suspicious death of one of his crew.

Helen Keller was not born deaf or blind. She was born with normal hearing and eyesight, but lost both abilities when she contracted scarlet fever or meningitis when she was 19 months old.

John F. Kennedy was not the youngest U.S. President. At age 43, he was the youngest elected President. However, Teddy Roosevelt was 42 when he became President after William McKinley was assassinated.

The quote, "Ask not what your country can do for you, ask what you can do for your country," was not originated by President **John F. Kennedy**. It was borrowed from a very similar 1884 statement by Supreme Court Justice Oliver Wendell Holmes.

President **John F. Kennedy** did not make a mistake when he said, "Ich bin ein Berliner" to a German crowd. Supposedly, the phrase translates to "I am a jam doughnut" and Germans thought this was funny. Not so—the phrase does indeed mean "I am a Berliner."

Robert Kennedy did not originate the statement, "You see things and you say, 'Why?' But I dream things that never were; and I say, 'Why not?'" It was written by George Bernard Shaw and borrowed by Kennedy for his 1968 presidential campaign.

General **Douglas MacArthur** did not originate the phrase, "Old soldiers never die, they just fade away." It was a refrain from a popular British army song.

Though "Machiavellian" now means calculating and deceitful, **Niccolo Machiavelli** was not evil. A character in his book <u>The Prince</u>, was an unscrupulous ruler, but Machiavelli never behaved like that character.

Marilyn Monroe did not have blonde hair. She started bleaching her naturally red hair a short time before she became famous.

Sir Isaac Newton was probably not hit by a falling apple. The first story published about this event appeared many years after his death.

President **Richard Nixon** did not say, "I am not a crook" as a result of the Watergate break-in and investigation. It was said many years earlier when he was questioned about his personal finances.

Sarah Palin did not say, "I can see Russia from my house." She said, "They're our next door neighbors and you can actually see Russia from land here in Alaska, from an Island in Alaska." The more famous quote was actually from Tina Fey in a skit on Saturday Night Live.

Pocahontas was not a young woman at the time she met John Smith. She was a young girl—about 10 years old.

Elvis Presley did not have black hair. It was sandy brown and he dyed it to look more like actor Tony Curtis.

Comedian **Richard Pryor's** near fatal burning was not a result of an accident while freebasing cocaine. Pryor, in a state of drug psychosis, tried to commit suicide by pouring alcohol on himself and lighting it.

Despite his depiction in the Shakespeare play, **King Richard III** was not a hunchback. Portraits and written descriptions from the time do not even hint the real king was a hunchback.

President **Franklin Roosevelt** did not originate the statement, "The only thing we have to fear is fear itself." Several authors made nearly identical statements well before Roosevelt made it famous.

General **William Tecumseh Sherman** did not say, "War is hell." He said, "There is many a boy here today who looks on war as all glory, but, boys, it is all hell."

Joseph Stalin was not Russian. The long-time premier of the Soviet Union was from Georgia, an entirely separate state from Russia.

President **Harry Truman** did not originate the quote, "If you can't stand the heat, get out of the kitchen." He borrowed the line from his chief military aide, Major General Harry Vaughn.

Mark Twain never said, "The coldest winter I ever spent was a summer in San Francisco." Only an obscure reference to a cold summer in Paris appears in any of Twain's writings.

French philosopher **Voltaire** never said, "I disapprove of what you say, but I will defend to the death your right to say it." The statement was a summation of one of his points made by essayist E. Beatrice Hall.

George Washington did not have artificial teeth made of wood. He used human and animal teeth inserted into plates of hippopotamus ivory.

George Washington did not wear a white wig. He powered his hair white.

George Washington was not born on February 22. According to the calendar in use at the time, it was February 11. His birthday changed when the British switched from the Julian calendar to the Gregorian calendar in 1752 and 11 calendar days had to be skipped. Washington decided to celebrate his birthday on February 22 because it was the true anniversary of his birth.

Not all of **George Washington**'s peers thought he was a great military leader. Thomas Jefferson, for example, said Washington was "a failure in the field—not a great tactician."

Food and Beverages

An **almond** is not a nut. It is a seed found in the fruit of the almond tree.

Apples are not native to North America. They were brought over from Europe.

Cut **apples** are not bad for you when they turn brown. The brown is a fine film that forms to keep bacteria from entering the apple. It has no taste and is harmless when swallowed.

There is no proof the artificial sweetener **aspartame** causes cancer, brain tumors, multiple sclerosis, or any other disease. Several studies have been conducted and the only significant negative effect is that aspartame stimulates the appetite and messes up your diet.

Bananas don't grow on trees. They grow on tall herb plants.

You're not likely to slip on a **banana peel**. It would take a whole bunch of banana peels to make you slip by accident.

Bombay duck, a popular Indian dish, contains no duck. It's a type of fish.

Boston baked beans are not from Boston. They're from Chicago.

Boston cream pie is not a pie. It's a cake.

Bottled water is no healthier or tastier than most tap water in the U.S. The little bit of processing that occurs adds no nutrients and takes away nothing dangerous. Blind taste tests have shown tasters generally rate tap water equal to bottled water.

The **Brazil nut** was not named after the country. The country was named after the nut, or more precisely, the tree called a "brazilwood."

Breadfruit is not a wheat product. It only has that name because the fruit tastes like bread when baked.

Brown eggs are no healthier than white eggs. The difference in color just indicates which breed of chicken laid the egg.

Buckwheat is not a type of wheat. It's the seed from a plant unrelated to wheat.

Buttermilk does not contain butter. It is what is left over when butter is made.

Butterscotch has nothing to do with Scotland. "Scotch" is an archaic term for marking or cutting something. Butterscotch referred to candy that was "scotched" into little pieces.

Eating **carrots** doesn't improve your eyesight. Eating any vegetable high in vitamin A helps maintain healthy eyesight, but it doesn't improve your vision.

Cashews aren't nuts. They're seeds.

Chili peppers aren't peppers. They are part of the nightshade family and are more closely related to tomatoes or eggplants. The mistake occurred when Christopher Columbus thought New World chilies were related to the spicy black pepper he was used to.

Chinese gooseberries aren't from China. They're from New Zealand. The name confused enough folks that exporters now call them kiwifruit.

Chock Full o'Nuts coffee contains no nuts. It's just coffee, and coffee beans aren't nuts. Its manufacturer, New York City's Chock Full o'Nuts restaurant chain, originally sold nuts.

Chocolate does not cause acne. Studies have shown chocolate and acne are unrelated.

Chocolate does not cause tooth decay. In fact, there is some evidence oils from chocolate may actually inhibit tooth decay.

Coca-Cola was not originally green. The rumor started because it was often sold in green bottles in the past.

A **coconut** is not a nut. It's a fruit.

The liquid found in the middle of **coconuts** is not coconut milk. It is coconut water. However, there is such a thing as coconut milk—it's what you get when you squeeze the meat of a coconut. The broader definition of "milk" does not require it come from an animal.

Coffee did not originate in South America. It originated in Africa and was exported to South America.

Coffee beans aren't beans. They're the pits of a fruit.

No corn is used when preparing **corned beef**. "Corn" originally referred to any "small hard particle," such as a grain of salt. Corned beef is beef cured in salt water.

The pastry known as a **Danish** did not originate in Denmark. It originated in Austria. In Denmark, it is known as "Vienna bread."

Decaffeinated coffee is not caffeine-free. It contains 5 mg per cup—an amount similar to a chocolate bar.

There is no such thing as a drink that causes **dehydration**. Coffee, alcohol, etc. may not hydrate you as much as water, but they do add water to your system.

Double-dipping chips does not spread germs significantly. While it's theoretically possible a few microbes could be added to the mix, there is already a substantial amount of bacteria floating around chips and dip.

Egg cream contains neither egg nor cream. It's made from milk, chocolate syrup, and seltzer water.

English muffins are not from England. They were created in the United States as a variation of English crumpets.

Fortune cookies are not served in China. They were invented in the United States.

The **French dip** sandwich did not originate in France. It originated in Los Angeles.

The **French dip** hasn't always been served "au jus," i.e., a cup of beef juice on the side for dipping. Originally, it was dipped before it was served.

French dressing did not originate in France. It is an American invention.

French fries did not originate in France. They probably appeared first in Belgium.

French toast is not from France. It was invented by an Albany, NY tavern owner named Joseph French.

Fried rice did not originate in China. It was first served in Indonesia.

Gelatin does not help make fingernails and toenails grow any faster or stronger. Studies have shown gelatin has no effect on the growth of your nails.

German chocolate cake did not originate in Germany. It was created by an Englishman named Sam German.

Grape-Nut cereal contains neither grapes nor nuts. It's primarily whole grain wheat flour.

Hawaiian pizza did not originate in Hawaii. It's just that pineapples are grown there.

Head cheese is not cheese. It's a jelly made with meat from the head of a cow or a pig.

Hollandaise sauce did not originate in Holland or any part of the Netherlands. The French created it.

Irish stew is unknown in Ireland. It's an American invention.

Italian dressing is not from Italy. Italians dress their salads at the table with olive oil, vinegar, and salt, but not as a pre-mixed vinaigrette.

Jordan almonds are not from Jordan. They originated in Italy.

London broil is not from London. It's unknown in England.

Mayonnaise does not spoil easily. Though often blamed when someone gets sick from an unrefrigerated sandwich, it's usually the chicken or tuna that goes bad. Mayonnaise is actually acidic enough that it deters food from spoiling.

Cows are not the most common source of **milk**. Around the world, more folks drink goat's milk.

Mincemeat usually contains no meat. It contains nuts, dried fruit, suet, spices, and brandy or rum.

Mussels that do not open when cooked are no less safe to eat. Mussels that are not fully cooked can be unsafe, but whether they are open or closed is not an indication of whether they're sufficiently cooked.

Not all **oranges** are orange-colored. Many are green or yellow when they ripen. To make sure they are orange when they go to market, growers spray green ones with ethylene gas to kill the chlorophyll. Yellow oranges are dipped into a red dye to make them appear orange-colored.

A **peanut** is not a nut. It's a legume.

Philadelphia Brand cream cheese is not from Philadelphia. It originated in New York City, and received its name because Philadelphia was once considered a center for top-quality food.

Pineapples are unrelated to either pine or apples. They were named by Christopher Columbus who thought they looked like pine cones and tasted like apples.

Pineapples are not native to Hawaii. They were imported to Hawaii from the Caribbean.

Potatoes did not originate in Ireland. They were originally from the Andes in South America and brought to Europe by Spanish explorers.

You can't bake a **potato** in a microwave. What you're doing is steaming the potato. The consistency of the cooked potato will not be the same.

Refried beans are not fried a second time. They're fried just once.

Reese's Peanut Butter Cups were not invented when a person eating peanut butter bumped into a person eating chocolate. That rumor has a very obvious source: a humorous 1970s TV commercial depicting this made-up event.

Rocky Mountain Oysters are not oysters. They're deep-fried bull testicles.

Russian dressing is not from Russia. Many years ago, caviar was included as an ingredient. Someone apparently thought that sounded Russian and named it accordingly.

The **Saskatoon berry** is not named after Saskatoon, Saskatchewan. The city is named after the berry.

Sauerkraut did not originate in Germany. It was originally from China, and likely introduced to Europe by Genghis Khan's troops in the 13th century.

Searing meat does not seal in the juices. Searing does enhance the flavor, but that's a result of proteins and sugars reacting to heat.

Tapping the top of a shaken **soda can** does not stop the soda from shooting or foaming out when opened. The only solution is to let the can sit, though you can reduce the pressure by opening the can very slightly.

Spanish food is not hot and spicy. It's kind of bland. It's Mexican food that can be hot and spicy.

Strawberries aren't berries. They're a different classification of fruit.

Sweet potatoes and yams are not the same thing. U.S. Supermarkets label sweet potatoes as yams, but yams are from a different family, are grown in a different part of the world, and do not taste the same.

Sugar does not rot teeth. The real culprits are the acids found in many sweet treats—the same acids found in many fruits and vegetables.

Sugar does not make children hyperactive. They often eat sugar at more excitable times, e.g., parties, but it isn't the sugar that revs them up.

Foods packaged with the label **sugar-free** are not completely free of sugar and do not necessarily have fewer calories. The label only means less than .5 grams of ordinary sugar are in a serving. Many of these foods have other forms of sugar, such as glucose or fructose.

The term **sushi** does not refer to raw fish. Sashimi is raw fish. "Sushi" refers to food prepared by mixing hot rice with vinegar and sugar.

Sweetbread is not sweet or bread. It's either the thymus of a young calf or the pancreas of an older calf.

Eating **turkey** is not the reason you feel sleepy after a Thanksgiving meal. Though there is a chemical in turkey that could theoretically have a drowsy effect, you would have to eat an enormous amount of turkey on an empty stomach. The real cause of that drowsiness is usually a combination of large quantities of carbohydrate-rich food and alcohol.

You should not thaw a **turkey** by letting it sit at room temperature. Salmonella bacteria grow rapidly at room temperature—thawing in the refrigerator over a longer period is a much safer method.

Twinkies don't remain fresh for years. They last a bit longer than other bakery products, but their shelf life is only 25 days.

Welsh rabbit contains no rabbit. And it's not Welsh. It's just melted cheese on toast.

White chocolate is not real chocolate. It contains neither chocolate liquor nor cocoa solids. It's a sugar confection flavored with cocoa butter.

Holidays

Boxing Day, a holiday that many countries celebrate on the first workday after Christmas, has nothing to do with the sport or throwing away empty Christmas boxes. It's the day folks give Christmas "boxes," i.e., gifts, to mail carriers and the like.

The very Christian Puritans weren't big fans of **Christmas**. They outlawed it in 1659 and fined anyone who celebrated it. They thought the celebration gave too much "liberty to carnal and sensual delights."

Christmas is not celebrated on December 25 because that was the day Jesus was born. He was likely born in the spring. That date was probably picked because it was the date of a pagan festival celebrating the arrival of winter.

Christmas candy canes are not in the shape of a "J" to represent Jesus. They were originally bent to represent shepherds' crooks, and are still popular because they hang well from tree branches and effectively silence whining children.

Cinco de Mayo is not Mexico's Independence Day. It's the anniversary of an important 1862 battle. Mexican Independence Day is September 16.

Cinco de Mayo is not particularly big in Mexico. The only major celebrations are in the village of Puebla where the 1862 battle took place. Cinco de Mayo is actually a bigger deal in the U.S. than in Mexico.

Easter did not originate as a Christian holiday, and does not coincide with the date Christ likely died. It began as a pagan holiday that celebrated the arrival of spring. The traditions of Easter eggs and the Easter bunny originally honored fertility and rebirth during the spring.

The **Fourth of July** did not begin as a holiday immediately after the American Revolution. Federal employees didn't get July 4th off until 1870. And even then, they weren't paid. That happened in 1941 when it was made a paid Federal holiday.

Halloween is not the second biggest holiday retail money-maker after Christmas. Its advertising campaign during September and October is now the second longest among the holidays, but its sales are still below Mother's Day, Valentine's Day, Easter, and Father's Day.

There are no documented cases of children being poisoned on **Halloween**. However, there have been a few instances where pins or needles were found in Halloween treats. No one has been seriously hurt, but a Minneapolis man was arrested in 2000 for passing out candy that contained needles.

May Day did not originate in any of the socialist countries that celebrate its pro-labor message. It originated in the United States. Soon after labor unions tried to establish an 8-hour work day on May 1, 1886, a demonstration turned deadly in Chicago's Haymarket Square. May 1 became an international day of labor solidarity to commemorate this event.

New Year's Day is not the deadliest day of the year in terms of automobile accidents. That honor goes to July 4th. However, it is the deadliest day for pedestrians, even ahead of Halloween.

Even though Julius Caesar established January 1 as **New Year's Day**, most of the Western world didn't adopt that date for a good part of the millennium. In fact, England and the colonies celebrated New Year's Day on March 25 until 1752. This is why George Washington's birth year, considered 1731 at the time of his birth, was converted to 1732. January 1 to March 25 became part of the following year, so his February birthday meant his birth year had to be converted.

The official **Oktoberfest** in Munich, Germany does not begin in October. It begins in September and ends on the first Sunday in October.

There is no Federal holiday called **President's Day** that honors both Washington and Lincoln. It's still technically "Washington's birthday." There's never been a Federal holiday for Lincoln's birthday. Many states used to celebrate Lincoln's birthday, but that tradition ended when Martin Luther King Day was added in 1986.

Rudolf the Red-Nosed Reindeer apparently was not a male. Only female reindeer keep their antlers through the winter.

The modern image of **Santa Claus** as a rotund man with a white beard dressed in red was not created by Coca Cola as part of a 1930 ad campaign. This popular Santa Claus image was well established in the 19th century.

St. Patrick was not born on March 17. That was the date he died.

St. Patrick was not Irish. He was from England and helped establish the Christian Church in Ireland later in his life.

There is no evidence **St. Patrick** chased the snakes out of Ireland, or, for that matter, even saw a snake in his life. There were no snakes in Ireland when St. Patrick moved there in the 5th century.

Suicide rates do not increase during the Christmas season. In fact, they decrease a bit. The highest rates are in the summer.

Thanksgiving has not been continuously celebrated since the original feast in 1621. It wasn't celebrated yearly until the 19th century.

The period around **Valentine's Day** is not the most popular for wedding proposals. The period around Christmas Day and New Year's Day is more popular.

Xmas is not a modern, disrespectful term for Christmas. The first letter in the Greek word for Christ is "chi," which is represented by a symbol similar to the letter "X." Folks have been calling it Xmas for centuries.

Human Body

It isn't only men that have an **Adam's apple**. Women also have this enlarged cartilage over the outside of their larynx. It's just larger in grown men.

There is no relationship between **Alzheimer's disease** and exposure to aluminum. This is a myth that probably resulted from the fact both words begin "al."

People from **ancient times** were not necessarily shorter and did not necessarily live shorter lives. Nobles who had good diets were generally as tall as people today, and lived as long as people today. It's only because of the limited diets and medical care in ancient times that height and longevity were significantly stunted.

Antiperspirants do not stop sweat by blocking sweat pores in the skin. Antiperspirants contain aluminum, which short circuits the body's perspiration system.

Despite the sales pitches of mouthwash manufacturers, **bad breath** has very little to do with what's going on in your mouth. The oils of certain foods, e.g., garlic, come in contact with your lungs through the bloodstream, causing, literally, bad breath.

Baldness is not genetically passed through mothers only. Like most genetic traits, it can come from either side of the family.

Getting a **base tan** at a tanning parlor will not decrease your chances of skin damage on your vacation. First, tanning lights will cause similar damage. Second, prolonged exposure to the sun can damage your skin even if you have "pre-tanned."

There really is no such thing as a **beer belly**. Studies have shown there is no link between beer drinking and stomach size. A particularly large belly is a result of genetic disposition or a general lack of healthy behavior, i.e., lack of exercise and overeating.

Human **bones** are not white. They range in color from beige to light brown. Skeleton bones only appear white after they are boiled clean.

In proportion to the size of their overall body, humans do not have the largest **brains**. That distinction goes to the ant. An ant's brain is 6 percent of its body weight, while a human's brain is 2 percent.

Wearing **briefs** does not cause sterility. Theoretically, a little wiggle room in that area might help maintain room temperature, which is ideal for sperm production. However, the effect is very minor. You can wear tighty-whiteys all day long and expect no loss in reproductive capability.

Chewing gum does not take seven years to pass through the body. In fact, it passes through the body at the same speed as any other swallowed item.

Cigarettes don't calm your nerves. While it's true smokers feel as though cigarettes calm their nerves, smoking a cigarette only reduces the feelings of withdrawal, i.e., feelings that never bother non-smokers.

People that are **color blind** rarely see no color at all. They usually can't discriminate between just a few similar colors. It's rare an individual literally sees in grayscale, i.e., only in shades of black, white, and gray.

Copper bracelets don't cure arthritis. This is a very old hoax proven false long ago.

Cracking your knuckles does not cause arthritis. However, cracking your knuckles a lot can cause some hand swelling.

You will not get **cramps** because you swam within an hour of eating. And even if you did, the cramps would be so minor they would not increase your risk of drowning.

The human body does not lose 21 grams upon **death**. This notion comes from a flawed experiment over 100 years ago and has been proven false.

Decapitation, e.g., execution by a guillotine, does not cause instant death. The head can remain conscious for up to 15 seconds after it is severed.

There are no **double-jointed** people. Some people just have looser ligaments than others.

Mixing **Drano** with the urine of a pregnant woman does not indicate the sex of the unborn child. It only indicates you're pretty gullible.

Those things on each side of your head are not **ears**. They are technically "pinnas." The ear is the internal organ that makes hearing possible.

You don't need to drink **eight glasses of water a day** to stay healthy. You receive most of your water requirements from food, especially fruit.

Sitting too close to the TV doesn't hurt your **eyes**. However, watching too much TV, from any distance, is related to obesity and poor performance in school.

Reading in poor light does not damage your **eyes**. It will cause eye fatigue, making it temporarily tougher to read, but it does not cause permanent damage.

It's not the end of your **fingernail** that continually grows. The growth occurs under your skin and pushes the whole fingernail out. What you clip today has been around for several months.

Fingernails and hair do not continue to grow for a few days after death. Because bodies dehydrate after death, the skin tightens, making the nails and hair appear longer.

There's nothing funny about being hit on the **funny bone**. In fact, it's not even a bone that's been hit. It's the ulnar nerve. "Funny bone" is a pun based on the nerve's proximity to the humerus bone and its sound-alike "humorous."

Despite the phrase **gray matter**, human brains are not gray. They are pink. They turn gray when removed from the body's blood supply.

Sufferers of **hay fever** are not allergic to hay and do not suffer from a fever. They are allergic to various pollens, but none of them are from hay. And a fever is not one of the cold-like symptoms hay fever sufferers tend to experience.

Hair does not become gray as people age. As we get older, hair often grows in without pigment. This makes the individual hair white. Gray hair is the mixture of hair with color and white hair.

Hair does not grow in thicker and faster after it has been shaved. It will grow at the same thickness and speed as if it hadn't been shaved.

Hangnails aren't nails that hang. Hang comes from the old English word "ang," which means "pain." They are nails that hurt.

There has never been a documented case of a drugged, unconscious person having their **harvested organs** sold on the black market. This is an urban legend perpetuated on the Internet.

In cold weather, you don't lose most of your body heat through your **head**. Wearing a hat will make you feel warmer, but it doesn't keep heat from escaping any more than covering other parts of your body.

Headaches typically have nothing to do with the brain. Head pain is almost always related to surfaces outside of the skull, such as muscles contracting on the scalp or neck, blood vessels constricting on the scalp or face, or inflammation of the naval sinuses.

Your **heart** is not on the left side of your chest. Because of the way it's positioned in the chest, doctors can hear it better on the left side with their stethoscope. But more of your heart is located on the right side of your chest.

The sound doctors hear when they listen to your **heart** is not your heart beating, i.e., rhythmically contracting. It's the sound of the valves within your heart slapping shut.

Heartburn has nothing to do with the heart. It occurs when gastric secretions ("reflux") irritate the esophagus, roughly in the area near your heart.

Not all **identical twins** are of the same sex. There have been three known cases where a boy and a girl were born from the same egg.

The ideal **length of sleep** for adults is not eight hours. Studies have shown adults who sleep six or seven hours a day tend to live longer than those who sleep eight hours or more.

Your **limbs** don't fall asleep. An arm or a leg can feel numb when a major nerve has been pinched towards the bone, but this is unrelated to sleep.

The **mouth** is not the most sensitive part of the human body. Eyeballs have considerably more nerve endings than your mouth.

Contrary to common belief, drinking milk does not produce **mucus**. Some folks suggest you avoid milk when you have a cold because it will worsen nasal congestion. This is just not true—milk is no more related to mucus than any other fluid.

Humans do not have two **nostrils**. They have four. Two are hidden inside the head and connect the throat to the nose. They allow breathing through the nose.

Reports of people **over 110 years old** are grossly exaggerated. Biologists believe the maximum age of humans is about 110. Most folks purported to be over 110 do not have birth certificates or any other accurate historical record.

The name we give our smallest finger, the **pinkie**, did not originate as a cute child's nickname for the digit. It comes from the Dutch word, "pinkje," which means, "little finger."

Mothers and their fetuses do not share blood during **pregnancy**. Nutrients are shared via common access to the placenta, but the mother and fetus retain separate circulatory systems throughout the gestation process.

Men don't have one less **rib** than women. The Bible says Adam gave up a rib when Eve was created, but apparently this generous act of sharing did not continue across generations.

Ringworm is not a worm and was not caused by a worm. It's a type of skin fungus that grows out from a circle, and looks somewhat like a ring.

Schizophrenia is not the same thing as having multiple personalities. A person with schizophrenia most often suffers from a separation from reality, thought disturbances, and social withdrawal. They rarely demonstrate more than one personality. Those who experience more than one personality suffer from a different illness, called multiple personality disorder.

Referring to twins connected together as **Siamese twins** is incorrect. A famous pair of twins born in 1811 in Siam helped created this misnomer. This condition, of course, is unrelated to the twins' nationality—the correct term is "conjoined twins."

That shriveled look your **skin** takes when you've been in water for a long time is not shrinkage. Your skin takes on some of the water you've been soaking in, enlarging wrinkles you already have.

You don't feel with the outside layer of your **skin**. It's the second layer where tactile messages are received. The outside layer, which is constantly replacing itself, has no sensitivity.

The **skull** is not one bone—it consists of 22 separate bones. As children grow older, these bones fuse together and remain intact. "Soft spots" in the skull of infants are places where the bones haven't fully fused together.

"Never wake a person **sleepwalking**" is not good advice. The risk of the person getting injured far exceeds the short-term disorientation the person will encounter when woken.

The sound you hear when you **snap your fingers** is not a result of your forefinger striking your thumb. It's the sound of your forefinger striking the base of your thumb afterwards.

You can't repair **split ends** in your hair through a hair conditioning product. The only way to get rid of them is to trim your hair.

You don't digest food in your **stomach**. It's only being prepared for the actual digestive process that will take place in the small intestine.

Sweating a lot in a sauna is not an effective way to lose weight. You only experience a short-term decrease in the amount of fluid in your body. The weight returns as soon you re-hydrate.

Tapeworms generally do not lead to significant weight loss. Most tapeworms go unnoticed until sections of the tapeworm are passed, and there is very little, if any, weight loss.

Targeted toning exercises don't work to reduce fat in particular areas. For example, "ab machines" alone will not reduce fat in your abdominal muscles. Lots of any exercise can cause general weight loss, but you can't target specific areas.

Our ability to **taste** is not the primary factor in how we differentiate between foods. Our sense of smell is more important. Our taste buds are only effective in discerning very broad taste sensations, e.g., bitter, sweet, sour.

Particular tastes are not confined to specific parts of the **tongue**. The various tastes can be detected on all parts of the tongue. The supposed "tongue map," which shows the locations of different types of taste are your tongue, is based on a discredited research paper written in 1901.

The **tongue** is often cited as the strongest muscle in the body, but there's nothing to support this claim. Many muscles, particularly the gluteus maximus and the quadriceps femoris, can "lift" considerably more weight. Plus, the tongue isn't just one muscle—it's made up of 16 muscles.

Not all individuals with **Tourette's syndrome** swear involuntarily. The syndrome causes involuntary motor and vocal tics, but only about 10% of those with the disease swear.

Despite the claim on Snapple bottle caps, the average person doesn't **walk** 18,000 steps a day. The average is more like 3,000. Many wellness programs consider 10,000 steps a day an admirable goal.

You can't get **warts** by touching toads. They are caused by viruses unique to humans. Those bumps on toads are completely unrelated to warts.

Inside America

The U.S. Flag Code does not say the **American flag** should be burned if it touches the ground. The code says the flag is not to touch the ground and damaged flags should be burned. However, having touched the ground is not in the code's definition of damage.

The **Black Hills** of South Dakota aren't hills. Their size classifies them as mountains.

Buffalo, New York was not named for the American bison called a "buffalo." The name is a result of increasing mispronunciation of the original French name, Belle Fleume.

California is not the U.S. state most prone to earthquakes. The winner of that honor is Alaska.

Even excluding Alaska, the United States is not completely below **Canada**. Twenty-eight states are at least partially above Lake Erie's Middle Island, Canada's southernmost point. Fourteen states are completely above Middle Island.

Chicago did not receive its nickname, the "Windy City," because of its weather. A New York newspaper writer used the term in 1893 to insult Chicago's politicians after they endlessly boasted about their World's Fair.

There is no such thing as the **Congressional Medal of Honor**. It's just the Medal of Honor. It was created in 1862 by Congress, but Congressional is not part of the name.

Dixie, the nickname for the American South during the Civil War, did not come from the Mason-Dixon Line. It likely came from the song, "I wish I was in Dixie's Land." The song was part of a pre-Civil War minstrel show featuring a character named John Dixie.

Diamond Head, the volcanic rock formation overlooking Honolulu, Hawaii, isn't called that because it looks like a diamond. It is called Diamond Head because 19th century British sailors thought the

63

mountain-side was covered with diamonds. What they found were calcite crystals that only looked like diamonds.

The **easternmost state** in the United States is not Maine. It's the same state as the westernmost—Alaska. Some of the Aleutian Islands lie on the west side of the International Dateline, so they are officially in the Eastern Hemisphere.

The **East River** in New York is not a river. It's backed up ocean water.

The official motto of the United States is not **e pluribus unum**. It was for many years, but was replaced in 1956 by "In God we trust."

There are not **fifty states** in the United States. There are 46. Kentucky, Massachusetts, Pennsylvania, and Virginia consider themselves "commonwealths."

The **Golden Gate Bridge** in San Francisco is not gold colored. Its official color is "International Orange."

The **Grand Canyon** is not the deepest canyon in the United States. The deepest is Hell's Canyon in Idaho and Oregon.

Grand Central Station is not the name of the railway station in New York City. The name is Grand Central Terminal.

Kansas City, at least the one you usually think of, is not in Kansas. The bigger version with the football and baseball teams is in Missouri. The smaller version is in Kansas.

The **Mason-Dixon Line** was not created as a means for differentiating between the North and the South during the Civil War. It was created in the 1760s when surveyors Charles Mason and Jeremiah Dixon helped establish the border between Maryland and Pennsylvania. Politicians later referred to the line when describing the northern and southern parts of the country.

The name of the Alaskan city, **Nome**, did not originate from Inuit language. It came from a mistake. A map maker misread a ship's officer's scribbling, and decided "Name?" must be "Nome."

Chicago's **Northwestern University** is not in northwestern Illinois or northwestern Chicago. Before the Far West was explored, Illinois was considered part of the "Northwest Territory."

The U.S.'s **paper money** is not made from paper. It is 25% linen and 75% cotton.

The folks known as **Pennsylvania Dutch** were not from the Netherlands. They were from Germany. Dutch, in this case, is a variation on the German word for German, "Deutsch."

It's not true that only people born in the United States are eligible to be **president**. Naturalized citizens, i.e., immigrants who are granted citizenship, are not eligible, but a foreign-born child of a U.S. citizen travelling or working abroad is eligible.

Bashing of the **president** is not a new phenomenon. The media and Internet blogs are often blamed for the ridicule directed at recent presidents; however, all presidents have endured considerable scorn during their tenure. Lincoln was teased about his looks. Grant was called a drunk. Even Washington's opponents called for his impeachment during his presidency.

The **Rio Grande** and **Rio Bravo** rivers are not two distinct rivers. They are just two names for the same river that separates Texas and Mexico. Rio Grande is the name in the United States and Rio Bravo (actually Rio Bravo del Norte) is the name in Mexico.

The eagle depicted in the official **Seal of the President of the United States** does not look a different direction during wartime. It is a common belief the eagle looks at the arrows in its right talon while the country is at war, and at the olive branch in its left talon when the country is at peace. In reality, the eagle is always turned towards the talon with the olive branch.

The **Sierra Nevada Mountains** are not in Nevada. They are almost entirely in California.

The **southernmost state** is not Florida. It's Hawaii, which lies about 200 miles south of the Florida Keys.

The actual name of the **Statue of Liberty** is not the Statue of Liberty. It's "Liberty Enlightening the World."

St. Augustine is not the oldest community in the United States. It is the oldest predominately inhabited by European settlers. The oldest known community is the Pueblo Indian village of Acoma, New Mexico, built approximately 500 years before St. Augustine.

Texas does not have a special exemption that allows its state flag to be flown at the same height as the American flag. The U.S. and Texas flag codes don't mention anything like this.

The United States did not discontinue the printing of **two dollar bills**. The Treasury Department printed 61 million two dollar bills in 2005 alone. They are rarely used because businesses have trouble convincing consumers they are legal tender.

The **United Nations** is not located in the United States. Its New York City location is officially international territory.

The **U.S. Air Force** is not the military branch with the most aircraft. That honor goes to the U.S. Army, which maintains a large number of planes and helicopters for transporting soldiers and supplies.

There are no denominations of **U.S. currency** above $100 bill in circulation. Larger bills, e.g., the $1000 bill, were discontinued in 1969.

The **U.S. Postal Service**'s motto is not "Neither snow nor rain nor heat nor gloom of night stays these couriers from the swift completion of their appointed rounds." It actually comes from the 500 B.C. Persian mail service. People assumed the quote belonged to the U.S. Postal Service after it was inscribed on the New York Post Office building.

West Virginia is not really west of Virginia. Parts of Virginia are west of West Virginia's western border.

The **White House** didn't get its name after it was repainted white during the War of 1812. While it was repainted after it was burned by the British, it had always been white. Many referred to it as The White House long before the War of 1812.

Inventions

The **abacus** was not originally from China. It mostly likely originated in ancient Egypt.

The Wright brothers did not invent the first **airplane**. Their historic flight was the first manned, controlled, powered, and sustained flight of a heavier-than-air craft, but airplanes, e.g., gliders, were around for several years before the Wright Brothers' flight.

Aluminum foil was not invented to keep food fresh in the refrigerator. The R.J. Reynolds Tobacco Company created it as a cheaper way to keep their cigarettes fresh.

The **assembly line** was not invented by Henry Ford. It was first used by car maker Ransom E. Olds and later improved by Ford.

The **automobile** was not invented by Henry Ford or any other American. It was a gradual process that largely took place in Europe. The most significant event was the invention of the internal combustion engine by Nikolaus Otto and Gottlieb Daimler in 1876. Daimler, and Karl Benz, produced motorized automobiles in Europe nine years before the first American car was built in 1894 by Elwood Haynea.

The **bagpipe** did not originate in Scotland. It first appeared in the Middle East.

The **bikini**, or the two-piece swim suit, is not a recent invention. Women in two-piece suits can be found in ancient Greek paintings.

The **Bowie knife** was not invented by, or even named for, the famous frontiersman at the Alamo, James Bowie. It was invented by his brother, Rezin Pleasant Bowie.

Chemist Robert Bunsen did not invent the **Bunsen burner**. It was invented by Michael Faraday, and then improved by Peter Desaga, a student of Professor Robert Bunsen at the University of Heidelberg.

Buttons were not invented as fasteners for clothes. They were used as clothing ornaments as far back as 2000 BC. But they didn't fasten clothes until the 14th century.

Champagne was not invented by the French. It was invented by the British.

John Pemberton, the inventor of **Coca Cola**, did not make millions from his product. He sold the rights for $350 soon after he invented it.

Eli Whitney did not invent the **cotton gin**. He was just the first to obtain a patent.

The **dishwasher** was not invented to make dishwashing easier. It was invented to reduce the number of breakages caused by servants.

Elisha Otis did not invent the **elevator**. He invented the brake system that made elevators feasible in larger buildings.

The **fax machine** was not invented in the late 20th century. A patent for a fax machine was first awarded in 1843. The device was improved and a version was sold in 1861—several years before the introduction of a workable telephone.

Thomas Crapper, a 19th century Englishman, didn't invent the **flush toilet**. Flush toilets were used as far back as 2000 BC. However, Mr. Crapper made important contributions, including the floating ballcock.

Though it was named for him, the **guillotine** was not invented by Dr. Joseph Guillotine. The French originally called it the Louison because it was invented by Dr. Antoine Louis. Dr. Guillotine, an anatomy professor, was a major advocate of the device because he thought it was more humane than other forms of capital punishment.

Handkerchiefs were not invented for blowing one's nose. They were originally used for waving around in an elegant and dignified manner. It took about 300 years before someone figured out it was a handy target for the owner's stuffed nose.

The **light bulb** was not invented by Thomas Edison. Several inventors, including Humphry Davy, John W. Starr, and Heinrich Goebel, created forms of electric light prior to Edison. Edison's claim to fame is he made the light bulb commercially viable.

Vyacheslav Molotov did not invent the **Molotov cocktail**. These makeshift bombs were so named because Finnish soldiers threw them at Soviet Foreign Minister Molotov and his soldiers.

Monkeys had nothing to do with the naming of the **monkey wrench**. It's named after its inventor, Charles Moncky. Consistent misspelling led to a permanent change.

Thomas Edison didn't invent the **motion picture**. Several inventors, especially Louis Alme Augustin le Prince, played a more important role in its creation. Edison, however, did develop a film processor that made motion picture production commercially feasible.

The **parachute** was not invented for airplane safety. It was invented in 1783 by Louis-Sebastien Lenormand to save people who jump from a burning building.

Sir Alexander Fleming did not discover **penicillin**. Mold, the source of penicillin, was used as a healing ointment for centuries. In 1897, a doctor named Ernest Duchesne identified its antibiotic properties and cured typhoid in guinea pigs. It wasn't until 1929 that Fleming put its antibiotic properties fully to work.

Thomas Edison did not invent the **phonograph** to play music. Edison thought the telephone would be too expensive, so he worked on a "talking machine" that could produce sound messages that could be delivered to the intended office. Recorded music caught on later.

The **QWERTY** layout on typewriters was not created to speed up typing. The system spreads the most common letters across the keyboard to help keep the keys from jamming. In fact, it tends to slow the typist down relative to other keyboard arrangements.

Guglielmo Marconi did not invent the **radio**. Though Marconi's work was important, his role in the invention of the radio was exaggerated by

Mussolini's fascist regime in Italy. Much of Marconi's work was based on patents already established by Nikolas Tesla.

The **rickshaw** wasn't invented by an Asian. It was invented by an American missionary in Japan to get his wife around town quicker.

John Montagu, the Earl of Sandwich, didn't invent the **sandwich**. The idea of meat between two slices of bread existed before the birth of Christ. The sandwich, however, was named for him.

Elias Howe did not invent the **sewing machine**. Walter Hunt invented a similar machine 12 years earlier but never applied for a patent. However, Howe didn't simply obtain the patent because of the opportunity; he also made significant improvements.

Robert Fulton didn't invent the **steamboat**. Several individuals built working steamboats before Fulton launched his version. Robert Fulton's accomplishment was that he operated the first successful steamboat line.

James Watt did not invent the **steam engine**. He just improved upon it. Egyptians created a steam engine many centuries earlier.

Sudoku was not invented in Japan. It was invented in the 1970s by American Howard Garns, who sold his puzzles to a children's magazine.

Samuel Morse did not invent the **telegraph**. It was invented by a fellow named Joseph Henry. Morse invented the Morse code that helped popularize the telegraph.

Alexander Graham Bell didn't really invent the **telephone**. His contribution was a reliable telephone transmitter. In fact, he only beat a competitor to the patent office by two hours.

Galileo did not invent the **telescope**. That distinction goes to Hans Lippershey. Galileo built a more powerful version and pioneered its use in astronomy.

The **windmill** did not originate in the Netherlands. They were used in the Middle East hundreds of years before the Dutch first built them.

Language

Brides do not walk down the **aisle** at weddings. The middle section is the nave. The aisles are on the outside of the seating area.

Alumni are not necessarily the graduates of a particular school. The term includes all former students—even those who did not graduate.

Though **anti-Semitism** refers to prejudice against Jews, someone who is Semitic is not necessarily Jewish. Semitic refers to anyone who speaks a Semitic language, including Arabic.

The origin of the term **bellwether** has nothing to do with predicting the "weather." A wether is a castrated sheep. A bellwether was the lead sheep that wore a bell to warn the other sheep in the flock.

Cathedral isn't a name given to large, ornate churches. It refers to a "cathedra," the official throne of a bishop in his diocese. Cathedrals can also be relatively small and simple. And many churches are quite large and ornate, but are not cathedrals.

Celibate does not mean abstaining from sex. It means unmarried, which, believe it or not, was once synonymous with the absence of sex.

A **chauvinist** is not necessarily a person who treats women unequally. The term comes from Nicholas Chauvin, a French soldier who demonstrated mindless loyalty towards Napoleon Bonaparte. The term refers to someone who is blindly devoted to a cause—whatever cause that might be.

Chicken pox has nothing to do with chickens. The illness was called "gigan pox" in Old English, and eventually evolved into chicken pox. Gigan meant "itch."

Chinese is not the most common language in China. In fact, Chinese is not a language. The most common language in China is Mandarin, with Cantonese second.

Comrade was never a term used in reference to any citizen of the Soviet Union. The term only referred to members of the Communist Party.

Cop is not an acronym for "constable on patrol." It's a shortened version of "copper," describing someone who "cops," or "seizes," something.

The **cotton gin**, named by Eli Whitney, has nothing to do with alcohol. "Gin" is a shortened version of "engine."

The slang term for human waste, **crap**, is not a variation on the name of flush toilet entrepreneur Thomas Crapper. The term, based on the Old French word for waste, "crappe," preceded Mr. Crapper's plumbing career by many years.

Déjà vu is not simply the act of experiencing something a second time. It refers to a momentary sensation felt when a new experience has an eerily familiar feeling.

You don't **dial** someone's phone number. That was how you called someone with rotary phones, which are now obsolete.

Technically, a **dock** is not the landing you step onto when exiting a boat. That's a pier. A dock is the body of water where a pier sits.

The **dog days of summer** have nothing to do with lazy dogs in the summer. Romans thought Sirius, or the Dog Star, was closer in the summer and assumed it was causing the extra heat.

The term **86**, as in "Management 86'd our plans for a new drinking fountain," is not from 80-6, the supposed specifications for burying a murder victim 80 miles away and 6 feet deep. It probably originated in short-order diners as code for "nix," as in "stop serving that guy."

The phrase **freeze the balls off a brass monkey** did not come from a device on warships that held a pyramid of cannonballs. Supposedly, the lower cannonballs would contract in freezing temperatures, causing the cannonballs to come tumbling down. There was no device like this on warships—in fact, cannonballs were stored below deck and not in pyramids. There is no known valid explanation for this phrase.

A **French kiss** only goes by that name in the English speaking world. In France, it's known as an "English kiss."

That naughty **f-word** was never an acronym for "Fornication under Consent of the King." It's derived from the Middle Dutch word "fokken," which means "copulate."

Golf is not an acronym from the phrase "Gentlemen Only, Ladies Forbidden." It likely originated from "goulf," a Scottish verb meaning "strike," as in "strike the ball."

Guerilla warfare has nothing to do with gorillas. The word guerilla is from "guerra," the Spanish word for "war." Guerilla means "little war."

That round object above the head of saints and angels in paintings is technically not a **halo.** A halo is the general name for a round luminosity, such as the light around the sun in an eclipse. The correct name for a radiance above a holy figure's head is a "nimbus."

In Arabic culture, a **harem** does not refer to a man's wives or mistresses. It refers to an area of the household that can only be entered by females, including family, guests, and servants. Because some polygamous men had multiple wives in their harems, Western Culture misunderstood the term and changed its meaning.

The word **hooker** has nothing to do with Joseph Hooker, a Civil War general who supposedly hired prostitutes to entertain his soldiers. The term is probably based on the prostitutes who worked in the Corlear's Hook area of New York City in the early 19th century.

In its original language of Inuktitut, **igloo** does not mean a "snow house." It refers to all types of houses.

Inflammable is not the opposite of flammable. Both mean "easily set on fire." Nonflammable is the correct word for "not burnable."

IOU does not stand for "I owe you." It stands for "I owe unto" and was originally followed by the name of the person owed money.

A **labyrinth** is not the same thing as a maze. While there are many wrong directions you can go in a maze, a labyrinth only has a single path that travels directly to the finish.

That doughnut-like flotation device found on ships is not, technically, a **life preserver**. It is called a "ring buoy." Strictly speaking, a life preserver is what most folks call a life jacket.

The distress signal, **Mayday**, has nothing to do with the May 1 commemoration of spring's arrival or labor unions. It's from the French word, "m'aidez," which means "help me."

Mind your p's and q's does not refer to "pints and quarts." Supposedly, the phrase originated when bartenders tracked customer's tabs by marking a "p" (for pint) or a "q" (for quart) on the wall. But, in truth, pubs weren't yet serving beer in pints and quarts when this phrase first appeared. The phrase probably started when teachers advised students to be careful with these two letters in the alphabet—the lower case versions are mirror images of each other.

The word **nylon** does not come from a combination of New York and London, the two cities where it was introduced. Nylon is a modification of a name manufacturers had considered earlier: "No Run."

There is no such thing as **paper mache**. The correct name is papier-mâché.

A **parkway** is not a place to park—it's another name for an avenue. The term originally referred to roads with park-like landscaping.

They don't use **plastic** in plastic surgery. The word "plastic" comes from a Greek word meaning "to mold."

Posh is not an acronym for "Port Outward, Starboard Home," from rich European travelers who insisted on sun-free accommodations on their trips to and from India. "Posh" was a word for a "dandy" long before European trains traveled to India.

There is no rule in grammar that says you shouldn't end a sentence with a **preposition**. Doing this may sound a little less formal, but it doesn't break any rules—at least that I know of.

Prodigal, from the Biblical story about the "Prodigal Son," does not refer to someone who travels and then returns home. The term refers to someone who is wasteful. The son in the Bible story returned home after he wasted all of his money.

The proof is in the pudding is not correct. The correct wording is "The proof is in the taste of the pudding."

The phrase **the rabbit died** is an inaccurate description of the now obsolete procedure that determined whether a woman was pregnant. The test showed whether the ovaries of a rabbit changed after they were injected with the woman's urine. However, no rabbits died because they were injected with the urine. All of the rabbits died because it was necessary to euthanize them before inspecting their ovaries.

Romance languages are not called that because they have anything to do with "romance," as in romantic relationships. In this usage, "romance" is derived from the Latin word for "Roman."

The phrase **rule of thumb** did not originate from a 15th century law that said a man was allowed to beat his wife with a stick no thicker than his thumb. There is no evidence such a law ever existed. In the days before an exact measurement was easily obtainable, a person's thumb was commonly used for measuring a wide variety of things.

Eskimos don't have hundreds of words for **snow**. Four is the maximum of the various Eskimo-Aleut languages. There are more variations, but only because these languages typically clump words, including adjectives and verbs, into longer hyphenated words.

SOS doesn't stand for "Save Our Ship," "Send out Sailors," "Stop Other Signals,' or anything like that. It's formed from the two simplest Morse code signals: three dots for "s" and three dashes for "o."

Spare ribs aren't called "spare" because there's a scarcity of meat on the ribs. "Spare" comes from the German word for a "spit," and describes how they are often cooked.

There's no grammar rule against **splitting an infinitive**. Great authors have done if for centuries.

Squaw is not derived from a Native American word for "vagina." Linguists believe it was derived from the term for "young woman." However, the term is still considered offensive because of the demeaning stereotype it portrays of Native American women.

Teton, as in the Grand Tetons, is not a synonym for mountain. It's from the French word for breast. French trappers, apparently suffering from too much isolation, named the Grand Tetons in the early 19th century.

If you completely change your mind about something, you don't do a **360**. You do a 180. Turning 360 degrees means you completely rotate around until you're facing the same direction from which you started. Turning 180 degrees means you're facing the exact opposite direction.

Tip is not an acronym for "To Insure Promptness." No one knows the origin, but word experts long ago ruled that one out.

Toadstools have nothing to do with toads. The first part of the name comes from "tod," the German word for "death." It refers to the potential fatal nature of these mushrooms.

Twilight doesn't only refer to the period of partial light right after sunset. It also refers to the period right before sunrise.

The term **weapons of mass destruction** is not all that recent, and didn't always refer to nuclear weapons. It was used during World War II in England to refer to bombs in general.

When Juliet asks, "O Romeo, Romeo! **Wherefore** art thou Romeo?" she is not asking where Romeo is. "Wherefore" means "why." Juliet is asking why Romeo has to be Romeo.

Wop, an ethnic slur directed at Italians, is not an acronym for "without papers" or "without passport." It is a derivation of "guappo," an Italian term for a man with a cocky attitude.

In "**Ye** Olde Gift Shoppe, "ye" should not be pronounced with a "y" sound. The "y" in "ye" was a printer's interpretation of an Old English symbol called the "thorn." It's pronounced like "th," so the correct pronunciation of "ye" should be "the."

Law

Laws that prohibit drinking on Sunday weren't called **blue laws** because they made people "blue." Nor were they printed and posted on blue paper. The term was probably derived from the term "bluenose," a derogatory term for someone who is rigidly moral.

It is not illegal to **burn** American currency. You can do it all you want.

If a first attempt at **capital punishment** fails, the condemned prisoner isn't entitled to go free. In the rare case this occurs, court orders require the job be finished, i.e., another attempt be made as soon as feasible.

A creative work does not require a **copyright** notice (or the symbol ©) to be protected from copyright infringement. The courts have ruled most privately created works are automatically protected as soon as they are created.

You are not protected from **copyright infringement** just because you're not making money. You're also not protected just by crediting the source. The originator of the work has the right to decide how the material is used.

In criminal cases, **corpus delicti** does not refer to the corpse. It refers to the "body of evidence."

Entrapment does not refer to any situation where police officers catch suspects by pretending they are not police. It only refers to enticing people to commit crimes they would normally not commit.

Not all **juries** have twelve members. Twelve was arbitrarily picked long ago, and is now used out of tradition in most criminal court proceedings. However, many lesser crimes are tried before 6-member juries.

Not all **juries** must be unanimous. In particular, civil trials usually do not require unanimity, and sometimes require only a majority.

Libel and slander are not the same thing. Libel refers to written defamation of an individual, while slander is a spoken defamation.

Supposedly an example of a frivolous lawsuit, the woman who sued **McDonald's** when she spilled hot coffee on herself was not awarded millions. After appeal, the original $2.7 million award was lowered to $480,000. It should also be noted McDonald's served coffee 20 degrees hotter than other restaurants, and the 81-year old victim required multiple skin grafts on her groin, thighs, and buttocks.

When products are **mistakenly advertised** below their actual price, there is no legal obligation to honor the lower price. All the company has to prove is that it was a legitimate typo.

Pink jail cells, or cells of any soft color, have no impact on offender aggressiveness. This idea was advocated in the 1970s. However, subsequent research indicated the room's color has no impact on inmate surliness.

There is no legal merit to the statement "**possession** is nine-tenths of the law." In fact, "possession" has very little to do with who is entitled to keep something. "Ownership" is the correct legal requirement. "Finders keepers" is just not true. If you lose something you own and someone finds it, you need not weep.

During **prohibition**, it was not illegal to drink, possess, or buy liquor. It was only illegal to manufacture, sell, or transport liquor.

No laws allow churches to give **sanctuary** to people wanted by the police. The last asylum laws were abolished in 1623 by England's King James I.

Despite claims in the documentary film **Scared Straight**, programs where prisoners confront and frighten juvenile offenders do not reduce the likelihood of those youths re-offending. Researchers have shown these programs have no positive effect.

Police do not always need a **search warrant** to search your home or car. While TV cop shows often suggest that police can get in trouble if they don't have a warrant, all they usually require for a search is "probable cause" at the time of the search.

There is no **statute of limitations** for murder cases. Most states have a statute of limitations in place for lesser crimes, but murder is always exempt.

In real courtroom trials, as opposed to those on TV, there really is no such thing as a **surprise witness**. The rules of discovery require evidence and witnesses be announced before the trial begins. It is difficult to introduce new evidence after the discovery process.

The lawyers for Dan White, the man who killed San Francisco mayor George Moscone and supervisor Harvey Milk, did not argue Twinkies caused White to commit the murders, i.e., the so-called **Twinkie defense**. They sighted White's increased interest in Twinkies and other junk food as evidence he was clinically depressed.

A **verbal agreement** is no less binding than a written one. However, a written agreement is much better because it is easier to prove in a court of law.

Literature

James Bond's favorite drink is not the vodka martini. Over the series of books, Bond opts for bourbon about three times as often as a vodka martini.

The popular story about **Hans Brinker**, the Dutch boy who plugged a hole in a dike with his finger, is neither true nor Dutch in origin. It was written in the United States in 1865 by Mary Mapes Dodge.

Lewis Carroll did not originate the phrase "mad as a hatter" in <u>Alice in Wonderland</u>. It was around much earlier than the book's release. The phrase originated from an actual problem—poisoning from mercury salts used by 19th century hat makers caused a certain amount of madness in many hatters.

It is not true **Cinderella**'s glass slippers were originally fur slippers in the original Charles Perrault story. Supposedly, a translation error led to the switch. Perrault really did describe them as glass slipper.

"Divine Comedy" was not **Dante's** name for his classic poem. He named it "Comedy." A translator added "divine" after Dante's death.

Alexandre Dumas likely did not write <u>The Three Musketeers</u>. He had several collaborators for the many books he wrote, and experts believe August Macquet probably wrote <u>The Three Musketeers</u>.

Frankenstein is not the name of the monster in Mary Shelley's book. It's the name of the doctor who creates the monster. The monster has no name.

The **Brothers Grimm** did not create any of the stories they published. The brothers wrote down old, popular stories they had heard.

Sherlock Holmes never wore a deerstalker hat, and never said, "Elementary, my dear Watson," in any of the books. Those two parts of the Holmes persona were added by stage or film actors.

The **Pulitzer Prize**, given for outstanding journalism, was not named after an outstanding journalist. It was named after Joseph Pulitzer, owner and editor of various newspapers that used sensationalism and tabloid journalism to sell newspapers.

The nursery rhyme, **Ring around the Rosie**, has nothing to do with the Great Plague of London in 1665, or any other bubonic plague. Lines, such as "Ashes to ashes, we all fall down," supposedly refer to dying victims of the disease. In actuality, the poem appeared more than two hundred years after the plague. And, for that matter, many of the poem's verses are clearly unrelated to plague or death, e.g., "Cows are in the meadow, Eating Buttercups, ah-tishoo, ah-tishoo, We all jump up!"

J. K. Rowling is not the name of the author of the Harry Potter books. The author's actual name is Joanne Murray. Rowling was her maiden name. J. K. was picked because she didn't want readers to know she was female.

Benjamin Franklin did not create the **Saturday Evening Post**. Though the magazine gave him credit for that achievement, Franklin died 30 years before the magazine was ever published. The only connection was that Franklin printed the Pennsylvania Gazette in the same building that eventually became the home of the Saturday Evening Post.

The title of **John Steinbeck's** The Grapes of Wrath was not incorrectly translated to "The Angry Raisins" in Japan. This is just a popular joke that eventually became an urban legend.

It is very unlikely **Bram Stoker** based the title character in his novel Dracula on the Romanian ruler known as "Vlad the Impaler." Though both Count Dracula and Vlad III of Wallachia were blood-thirsty bad guys, there are too many differences to suggest the novel's character was even loosely based on the real Vlad.

In the **Thin Man** book and movies, the lead character, detective Nick Charles, is not the "Thin Man." The "Thin Man" is a character that is talked about in the book.

Henry David Thoreau did not live in isolation in the woods while writing Walden. His retreat was very close to his home and village, which he visited nearly every day.

Mark Twain's <u>The Adventures of Tom Sawyer</u> (1876) was not the first novel ever written on a typewriter. The first was Twain's <u>Life on the Mississippi </u> (1883). This popular misconception began when Twain misidentified the correct book in a quote he offered for a typewriter advertisement in 1904.

There's no poem called **Twas the Night before Christmas**. Its real title is "A Visit from Saint Nicholas."

In the book **The Ugly American**, there is no discussion of rude and obnoxious American tourists. It refers to a good man who just happens to be homely.

The many **Webster's Dictionaries** available in your bookstore are not directly connected to the Noah Webster who created the first American dictionary. The name is not copyrighted, so many companies have taken the opportunity to cash in on the name.

The author **Tennessee Williams** was not from Tennessee. He was from Mississippi.

Medicine

Acne does not result from poor face washing habits. It's an inflammation under the skin, i.e., it's not caused by what's on your skin. In fact, after acne erupts, scrubbing can make it worse.

More often than not, **bed rest** is not a good choice for recuperation. Early mobilization is frequently the better choice. This is particularly true for back pain, but it's also good advice for many other medical problems.

It isn't only women that contract, and die from, **breast cancer**. Approximately 1700 men contract the disease each year, and 500 die from it.

Cancer does not cause more deaths than any other disease. Heart disease is still the winner.

Going out in **cold weather**, underdressed or with wet hair, doesn't cause a cold. Viruses cause colds. People get colds in the winter more often because they tend to stay inside—in closer contact with people carrying viruses.

A **compound fracture** does not necessarily mean more than one bone was broken. It means the skin was broken by the broken bone. A fracture with more than one break is called a "multiple fracture."

People with a cold or the flu are not most **contagious** before the worst symptoms appear. In fact, they are most contagious when the symptoms are at their worst.

There is no medical reason for a person to eat cookies and drink orange juice after **donating blood**. Folks who have given blood are not particularly dehydrated, low in blood sugar, or anything else that would require food and drink. On the other hand, it is a nice little reward.

Though depicted in movies like "Pulp Fiction," there is no medical treatment that includes stabbing a person in the chest with a syringe full of **epinephrine**. Emergency doctors, regardless of the urgency of the situation, inject epinephrine into a vein.

The adage **feed a cold, starve a fever** is not good advice. Both colds and fevers cause fluid loss, so drinking is required to prevent dehydration. And you should eat regular meals during colds and fluids so you don't get even sicker from a lack of nutrients.

It's very unlikely even a very high **fever** will directly cause brain damage. Meningitis can cause both a high fever and brain damage, creating the misconception that fever in general can damage the brain.

You can't catch the flu from a **flu shot**. You might have flu-like symptoms if you're allergic to eggs, or if you're later exposed to a different strain of flu, but the virus strains in a flu shot have been inactivated.

The **Hippocratic Oath** was not written by Hippocrates. The ideas were from him, but none of his writing survived. It was created by an unknown person several hundred years after his death.

No state requires doctors to take the **Hippocratic Oath** to obtain their medical license. Modern ethics codes have long replaced it.

Leprosy is not highly contagious. In fact, it rarely moves from one person to another. Doctors and nurses who work with leprosy sufferers rarely contract the disease.

Leaning your head back does not stop a **nosebleed** any quicker. That practice likely originated as a method for keeping blood off the nose-bleeder's clothes. Leaning slightly forward, with the nose pinched, is much better method for stopping the bleeding.

The **plague** was never transmitted from one person to another. Nor was it transmitted by bites from rats. It was transmitted by bites from rat fleas, looking for a new home after their host rat died.

Plastic surgeons do not work primarily on frivolous elective procedures to enhance beauty. The majority of the surgeries performed by plastic surgeons are related to the repair of burns, injuries, or congenital deformities.

Polio has not been completely eradicated. Several hundred cases exist in Nigeria and nearby countries.

A glass of **red wine** with dinner every night, even in moderation, is not necessarily good for your health. While it can theoretically reduce the risk of heart disease, that benefit is very minor and still outweighed by other potential health risks.

Salmonella was not named for the fish. It's named for Daniel Salmon, the man who first identified it. You're considerably more likely to get Salmonella from chicken than salmon.

There is no such thing as **stomach flu**. The influenza virus affects the respiratory system, not the digestive system. An upset stomach can be an additional symptom of the flu, but most illnesses called the stomach flu are actually food poisoning.

Stomach ulcers are not caused by stress or spicy food. They are caused by infectious bacteria.

Rust doesn't cause **tetanus**. It's caused by a bacterium found in dirt, which may or may not be introduced through contact with something like a rusty nail.

There is no such thing as **24-hour flu**. Having flu symptoms for only 24 hours likely means you had a form of food poisoning.

Tuberculosis is not a "lung disease" per se. It's an infectious disease that can affect any part of the body. It is more common in the lungs because the infectious bacteria enter through inhalation.

A jellyfish sting should not be treated with **urine**. Urine contains ammonia, which makes the sting even more painful.

Movies

Charles Boyer never says, "Come with me to the Casbah," in the film **Algiers**. The line was made famous by Looney Tunes character Pepe LePew.

Though advertised as a "true story," most of the events in the horror film **The Amityville Horror** didn't take place. While there was a murder in the house, the family that eventually bought the house fabricated all of the paranormal business.

The Charlton Heston film **Ben Hur** was not based on the Bible. It's based on the Lew Wallace novel that takes place in biblical times.

In real life, the title characters in **Butch Cassidy and the Sundance Kid** were not the leaders of their gang. They were followers of an outlaw nicknamed "Kid Curry," who planned and led the gang's bank and train robberies.

James Cagney never said, "You dirty rat," in any of his films. The line was made famous by impersonators.

Humphrey Bogart never says, "Play it again, Sam," in **Casablanca**. The closest to that quote is when Ingrid Bergman says, "Play it once, Sam, for old times' sake."

Movies are no longer made of **celluloid**. They were for years, but that form of plastic is highly flammable and decomposes quickly. It has been replaced by cellulose acetate.

Though Brandon Lee was killed during the actual filming of **The Crow**, that scene is not included in the movie. The whole sequence was edited out of the movie.

Bela Lugosi, as the title character in the 1931 film **Dracula**, never says, "I want to suck your blood." That line has appeared in so many vampire spoofs that many assume it was in the original film.

Though the film opens with the words "This is a true story," the film **Fargo** is not based on an actual incident. The Coen Brothers admit the script is a complete work of fiction.

Kevin Costner's character in **Field of Dreams** doesn't hear a voice say, "If you build it, they will come," suggesting fans would come if he builds a ballpark. The line is, "If you build it, he will come," referring to the return of his deceased father.

W.C. Fields did not originate the comment "Anybody that hates children and dogs can't be all bad." A fellow named Leo Rosten said it while introducing Fields at a banquet.

W.C. Fields's tombstone does not say, "All things considered, I'd rather be in Philadelphia." It simply says, "W.C. Fields, 1880-1946."

A **full-screen** CD doesn't provide the full image shown in the original movie. That's a "widescreen" version. The images on full-screen CDs are truncated so they can be shown on older televisions with squarer screens.

The actress who was completely covered with gold paint in the film **Goldfinger** did not die from asphyxiation. The makers of the film were worried this was a possibility so they left a bare spot on the actress's belly. However, it's not possible to die this way.

Cary Grant never said, "Judy, Judy, Judy," in any of his films. He does say, "Yes, Judy," a few times in "Only Angels Have Wings," but that's about it.

The Great Train Robbery was not the first feature film. It was considered a landmark film in 1903, but it was only 10 minutes—well short of feature length. Further, several films of that length or longer had appeared earlier.

Despite a famous newsreel shown throughout the world, **Adolf Hitler** did not dance a victory jig after Germany defeated France. This newsreel was doctored to make Hitler appear to be dancing.

Though frequently depicted in the movies, it's not possible for a person to **hold on to the roof of a speeding car**. Because there's virtually nothing to hold on to, you'll be unable to hang on at virtually any speed, particularly if the car turns even a slight amount.

The **Hollywood** sign on a hill above Hollywood was not built to salute the city or the movie industry. It was originally "Hollywoodland" and was built to advertise a housing development near the hill. The last four letters were later removed by the Hollywood Chamber of Commerce.

Hollywood, or even generally the United States, is not the world's leading producer of feature-length motion pictures. Over three times as many features are produced in India each year.

In the many **Laurel and Hardy** films and shorts, Ollie never turned to Stan and said, "Here's another fine mess you've gotten me into." The actual phrase was "another nice mess."

The first name of **Chico Marx**, the Marx Brother with an Italian accent, is not pronounced "Cheek-oh." It is pronounced "Chick-oh."

The original **Miracle on 34th Street**, the film about a little girl who believes in Santa Claus, was not intended as a "Christmas movie." It was released in July of 1947.

Contrary to the image depicted in the **Mutiny on the Bounty** films, the actual Captain Bligh was no worse than other British sea captains of the time. In fact, Bligh flogged 10% of his crew, compared to 25% aboard Captain Cook's ship. The mutineers' primary complaint was that Bligh didn't want to stick around and enjoy their newfound tropical paradise in Tahiti.

The look of Tinker Bell, from Disney's animated version of **Peter Pan**, was not based on Marilyn Monroe. Actress Margaret Kerry served as the model for Tinker Bell.

It is a common belief, even among some projectionists, that **silent film** characters appear to move faster because these films were shot at a slower speed (16 frames per second) than the speed of modern projectors (24 frames per second). This is not true. Many films in the silent era were intentionally sped up to make the action look fast. Unfortunately, many projectionists now only show silent films at slower speeds (16 frames per second), which can makes the action look much slower and less interesting than originally intended.

In the original Snow White story, the villain was an evil stepmother, not an evil queen. Disney's **Snow White and Seven Dwarfs** changed her relationship to Snow White because Walt thought stepmothers were already getting too much of a bad rap.

The evil queen in Disney's **Snow White and the Seven Dwarfs** doesn't say, "Mirror, mirror on the wall, who is the fairest of them all?" She says, "Magic mirror on the wall, who is the fairest one of all?"

The real von Trapp family, portrayed in the movie **The Sound of Music**, didn't escape the Nazis by sneaking away at night. They left openly on a train in broad daylight.

Movie makers didn't head to **Southern California** in the early 20th century because of the nicer weather. They relocated to get away from Thomas Edison's lawyers, who were busy suing anyone who infringed on Mr. Edison's movie camera patent.

Johnny Weissmuller, in 1932's **Tarzan, the Ape Man**, doesn't say, "Me Tarzan, You Jane." He points at himself and says, "Tarzan," and then points at Margaret O'Sullivan and says, "Jane."

Johnny Weissmuller did not produce **Tarzan**'s famous scream on his own. Sound department specialists mixed in the sound of a soprano hitting a high C and a hyena howling.

No ghost of a murdered boy appears in the background of **Three Men and a Baby**. It's a cardboard cut-out of actor Ted Danson intended for another scene. The stage crew didn't realize it was in the shot.

Marisa Tomei was not named Best Supporting Actress in 1993 because a drunken Jack Palance read her name by mistake. According to the Academy's policies, they would have interrupted the ceremony if something like that ever happened.

The name of the computer in **2001: A Space Odyssey**, Hal, was not a take-off on IBM. Supposedly, each letter was "one step ahead of IBM." HAL is an acronym of "Heuristically programmed Algorithmic computer."

Mae West doesn't say, "Why don't you come up and see me sometime," in 1933's "She Done Him Wrong." She said, "Why don't you come up sometime, and see me? Come on up, I'll tell your fortune."

Gunfighters never shot from the hip as shown in **Western films**. They shot at waist level with the arm extended and the elbow half bent.

The song "White Christmas" was not introduced in the 1954 film **White Christmas**. Irving Berlin wrote the song for the 1942 film "Holiday Inn." The film "White Christmas" was released to capitalize on the song's success during the 1940s and 1950s.

In **The Wizard of Oz**, you don't see a suicidal Munchkin hanging from a tree in the forest next to the Yellow Brick Road. That's a large bird— one of several animals brought in to add some color and life to the movie.

Music

The title of the **Allman Brothers'** album "Eat a Peach," released only three months after guitarist's Duane Allman's death, was not a reference to his fatal motorcycle accident. Contrary to rumors, Allman did not crash into a peach truck. The album's title is from an Allman quote: "Every time I'm in Georgia, I eat a peach for peace."

The **banjo** did not originate in the American South. English explorers described similarly-constructed "banjars" in Africa many years before the onset of slave trading.

There are no females in the rock group **Barenaked Ladies**. They're all males and usually clothed.

The **Beatles** never smoked marijuana in Buckingham Palace. The story actually came from John Lennon, but he was only joking.

The **Beatles'** song "Lucy in the Sky with Diamonds" was not named for LSD. According to John Lennon, it was a coincidence—it was based on a drawing his son drew and titled "Lucy in the Sky with Diamonds."

Mama Cass from The Mamas and Papas did not die from choking on a ham sandwich. She died from a heart attack related to her obesity.

Chopin's "Minute Waltz" was not written to be played in a minute. Chopin used the word "minute" to mean "small."

Aaron Copeland did not name his famous classical piece "Appalachian Spring." He originally named it "Ballet for Martha." Choreographer Martha Graham then renamed it "Appalachian Spring" when she turned it into a ballet.

Buddy Holly did not die in a plane named "American Pie." Supposedly, that's the inspiration for the title of Don McLean's song. The plane had no name.

The **English horn** is neither English nor a horn. It's a woodwind from Vienna.

Spain's **flamenco** is not a dance per se. It's an art form consisting of four elements: guitar, vocals, hand claps, and dance. Of the four, dancing is the least essential and the one most often left out.

Alan Freed, the 1950s Cleveland disc jockey and an early promoter of rock 'n' roll, was not the first to use that term. The first known use of "rock 'n' roll" was in a 1937 song, "Rock It for Me," sung by Ella Fitzgerald.

Handel's Messiah was not written for the Christmas season. It was intended for, and originally performed at, Easter celebrations.

No member of the band **Hootie & the Blowfish** is named "Hootie." The band's lead singer, Darius Rucker, is often mistakenly referred to as Hootie, but the name is from a friend who was never in the band.

Michael Jackson never bought the corpse of John Merrick, the 19th century deformed man known as the Elephant Man. In fact, the body no longer exists—only casts of some of his bones. And Jackson didn't even own those.

The band **Jethro Tull** includes no one named Jethro Tull. Jethro Tull was an 18th century Englishman who invented the seed drill. The fellow usually mistaken for "Jethro Tull" is lead singer Ian Anderson.

Francis Scott Key did not write the music to "The Star Spangled Banner." He originally wrote the lyrics as a poem, called "The Defense of Fort McHenry." Key later set the words to the music of a British drinking song called "Anacreon in Heaven."

The name of the rock band **Kiss** is not an acronym for "Knights in Satan's Service." Band members have joked about being devil worshippers during interviews, but their name has no secret meaning.

The rock oldie, **"Louie Louie,"** does not have dirty lyrics. Fans misinterpreted Kingsmen lead singer Jack Ely's poorly-recorded vocals.

Martin Luther did not write the Christmas carol, "Away in the Manger." It was written by James R. Murray and credited to Luther to help the spread of Lutheranism.

Charles Manson never auditioned for the Monkees. A Los Angeles DJ claimed he saw someone who looked like him at the auditions, but Manson was in jail at the time.

Rock star **Marilyn Manson** did not play Kevin's friend Paul on the TV show The Wonder Years. Though he looks like the actor who played Paul (Josh Saviano), Manson was too old to have played Paul.

Playing classical music for babies in the womb does not make them smarter. Called the **Mozart Effect**, studies debunked this myth long ago.

The scream you hear during the **Ohio Players**' "Love Connection" isn't the sound of a woman who was murdered at the recording sessions. A DJ noticed an odd scream in the background and made a snide remark on the air. The rumor spread, with several variations of how the woman was killed.

Roy Orbison was not blind. He just always wore sunglasses when performing.

Ozzie Osborne does not regularly bite the heads off live bats while performing. However, he did do it once by accident. He mistook a real bat for a plastic prop. When he was forced to undergo the uncomfortable treatment for rabies, he decided he would never do it again.

Peter, Paul, and Mary's hit song, "Puff the Magic Dragon," was not written about smoking marijuana. The song's author has said it's nothing more than a fantasy about a magical dragon.

Though each member of the **Ramones** used the last name Ramone, e.g., Joey Ramone, none was born with that name. They got the idea from Paul McCartney, who occasionally used the pseudonym Paul Ramon.

Rolling Stones guitarist Keith Richards never had his blood "replaced." He did receive treatment in 1973 to remove impurities from his blood. Richards exaggerated the story for fun.

Grace Slick, lead singer for the Jefferson Airplane, did not name her child "god." She was merely joking with a nurse at the hospital. Her daughter's name is "China."

Ukuleles did not originate in Hawaii. Portuguese sailors brought them to the islands.

Jack and Meg White, members of the rock group **White Stripes**, are not brother and sister. They were married at one time, but have been divorced since 2000.

The **Woodstock** music festival did not take place in Woodstock, NY. It was staged in Bethel, NY. The event was originally intended for Woodstock, but the organizers could not get the proper permits.

Many **woodwind instruments** are not made from wood. For example, the all-metal saxophone is a woodwind.

Frank Zappa was not the son of Mr. Greenjeans from "The Captain Kangaroo Show." The story spread after Zappa wrote the song "Mr. Green Genes," and later, "Son of Mr. Green Genes."

Frank Zappa never ate human feces as part of a "gross-out contest" during one of his concerts. As the late Zappa once said, "The closest I ever came to eating s**t anywhere was at a Holiday Inn buffet."

Odds and Ends

No one was ever killed because they were sucking a lollipop when their automobile **airbag** deployed. This story was just an email hoax.

Arabic numbers did not originate in Arabia. They originated in India and gradually spread to Arabia, and finally Europe.

In the Greek myth, **Atlas** was not sentenced to hold the Earth on his shoulders and eternally serve as the poster boy for virtually all books of maps. He was condemned to hold all of the heavens on his shoulders.

It is no easier to **balance eggs** on their end on the vernal equinox—usually March 21. It is equally difficult on all days of the year.

Cannonballs shot from 18th century warships did not explode. They killed enemy sailors by causing large splinters of wood to fly around the ship, lacerating anyone within their path.

There's no evidence **chastity belts** existed in the Middle Ages. Experts on the subject believe chastity belts first appeared in the 19th century as humorous novelty items.

A **chef** is generally not a cook. Chefs plan and coordinate the cooking of a meal, but they rarely cook.

The game of **Chinese Checkers** is not from China and does not use checkers. It's from England and uses marbles.

No lawyer successfully made an insurance claim for his box of **cigars** that were "destroyed in a series of small fires." The story is based on an old joke that has been around for years.

Divorce rates are not going up because of an increasingly secular society. For one, the average U.S. divorce rate has decreased since 1981. Second, studies have shown divorce rates are lowest among secular groups, e.g., atheists and agnostics.

The name of the popular Japanese video game about a gorilla is not **Donkey Kong** because its real name, "Monkey Kong," was misspelled in translation. The actual name is "Donkey Kong"—the creators wanted a name that suggested the gorilla was stubborn and foolish.

Dust in your house is not dirt particles that floated in from outside. It's mostly made up of dead human skin.

Contrary to what we see in movies and television, dropping a stick of **dynamite** typically does not cause an explosion. Older versions of dynamite that had leaked could explode unpredictably, but newer dynamite can only be detonated with a blasting cap.

Dynamite and TNT are not the same thing. They are both explosives, but the mixtures are very different. The primary ingredient in dynamite is nitroglycerine, while TNT contains a chemical compound called trinitrotoluene.

Using a standard **fireplace** will not make your home warmer. In fact, the draft of warm air out of the house will typically make your home colder.

People act no stranger during a **full moon**. Studies have shown crime rates, suicides, fights, emergency room visits, etc. are no greater when the moon is full.

No known navy or company has had a rule that the captain must **go down with the ship**. The captain is often the last to board a lifeboat because of his or her responsibility to make sure the crew and passengers are safe. But giving up one's life has never been required.

The style of marching called the **goose step** was not originated by the Nazis. It was used by Prussian armies in the 17th century.

Gun silencers don't eliminate the sound of a gun, or even reduce it to the nearly inaudible "phut" you hear in movies. A low caliber gun can produce 160 decibels. With a silencer, it still produces at least 120 decibels—the equivalent of a thunderclap.

Immigration does not hurt employment among existing citizens. In fact, it tends to help employment opportunities and increase productivity. Portions of the labor force can be negatively affected, but the overall impact on a community's work force is generally positive.

The **iron maiden**, a torture device in which victims were locked and slowly pierced to death with spikes, never existed. There was a coat made of wood used to humiliate transgressors in public called an "iron maiden," but it never included spikes.

Men do not have most of the wealth in the United States. Enough women have outlived their husbands that women now have the majority of personal wealth.

The **middle finger salute** did not originate when English archers taunted their French enemies at the Battle of Agincourt. Supposedly, the French threatened to cut off the "plucking" finger of captured English archers, who used bows made from yew trees. In defiance, the archers shouted "pluck yew" as they flashed their still intact middle finger. In fact, the middle finger salute was used as a derogatory gesture in Roman times long before this silly story would have taken place.

It is not true more **Monopoly** money is printed everyday than U.S. currency. The U.S. Bureau of Engraving and Printing prints about $700 million of cash everyday. The best guess is no more than $150 million in Monopoly money is printed daily.

The **most popular first name** in the world isn't John, Mary, Jason, or Brittany. It's Muhammad.

A **one-way mirror** is not literally a mirror on one side and a window on the other. The glass is covered with a thin layer of aluminum, allowing only a small amount of light to pass through in either direction. The trick is to light one room more than normal, and keep the adjacent room dark. Those in the darkened room can see through the glass because of the brighter light in the other room.

A **penny** dropped from a skyscraper won't kill a pedestrian. Because of its shape and the impact of wind, it will only sting the unlucky victim.

It's not true a **piece of paper** cannot be folded more than seven times. The guys on "Mythbusters" folded a piece of paper eleven times.

Pull tabs from aluminum cans, back when they were removable, never had redemption value for time on dialysis machines. Well-meaning folks often put paper bags next to vending machines to collect these tabs so they could be donated to people who couldn't afford dialysis. No such program existed. The pull tabs ended up in the trash.

You won't completely sink below the surface if you fall into **quicksand**. At most, about three-quarters of your body will sink. That said, it won't be particularly easy getting yourself out.

Ship captains do not have the power to marry folks at sea. The only exception is if they already have the legal right to marry someone while on land, e.g., they're an ordained minister.

The sound you hear when you put a seashell to your ear is not the **sound of the ocean**. It's the sound of blood rushing through the veins in your ear as it echoes within the shell.

Spanish fly is not Spanish, is not from a fly, and does not act like an aphrodisiac. It is extracted from beetles found throughout Europe, and can cause severe blistering, vomiting, diarrhea, and internal bleeding.

The way the rider's horse is standing in **statues** of military leaders doesn't always indicate how the rider died. Supposedly, two hooves on the ground means the rider died in battle; three hooves means the rider was wounded and died later; and four hooves means he died in peacetime. This convention was used for statues commemorating the Battle of Gettysburg, but is otherwise rare.

Steamrollers don't run on steam any more. Virtually all are propelled by diesel.

Pouring **sugar** into a car's gas tank will not destroy the car's engine. The idea was that the car's heat would caramelize the sugar. When the engine cooled down, it would turn into hard candy. This won't happen— the worst damage is that the car's fuel filters will need to be replaced.

Suicide rates are not highest among teenagers and young adults. Rates among those groups are fairly low compared to rates for older age groups.

The **swastika** symbol was not created by the Nazis. Several cultures, e.g., the Mayans, used a similarly shaped symbol many years before the Nazis adopted it as their own.

There is no chemical that can be poured into a **swimming pool**, causing the water to turn blue when someone urinates.

The **toilet seat** is not the dirtiest place in the house. In fact, the typical desk has approximately 400 times as many bacteria as a toilet seat.

There is no such thing as **truth serum**. No chemical, or concoction of chemicals, has been invented that will force a person to tell the truth.

There is no evidence pirates ever made anyone **walk the plank**. If they wanted to get rid of someone, they just tossed their victim overboard.

Wedding dresses were not originally white to represent purity and innocence. Wealthy families had white dresses made to show they could afford a dress that would never be worn again.

An airplane was not first to break the sound barrier. It was a **whip**. The crack of a whip is a small sonic boom, not leather hitting leather.

The small walkways on the roofs of some houses, known as **widows' walks**, were not created so wives could watch for the return of their sailor husbands. They were installed for greater access to chimneys for fighting fires.

There really are no **windmills** anymore. Many wind-powered turbines used to "mill" grain, but now they usually generate electricity, and should be called "wind-powered generators."

The **yo-yo** did not originate as a weapon. There's no evidence it's been anything but a toy.

Zombies aren't just monsters made up by folks in the movie industry. There are scientifically validated stories about Haitians who were kept alive by Voodoo sorcerers. Near-lethal dosages of tetrodotoxin and/or datura into the bloodstream have apparently left some individuals in a near-death, trance-like state for several days.

Places around the World

Angel Falls in Venezuela is not called that because it's heavenly or spiritually-inspiring. It was named after Jimmy Angel, an American bush pilot who flew customers close to the falls.

The capital city of Thailand is not **Bangkok**. That name has not been used for over 200 years in Thailand. The correct name is Krung Thep, which is actually an abbreviation of a 152-letter name.

The **Black Forest** is a mountain range. True, it's a wooded mountain range, but the name actually refers to the mountains.

Kissing Ireland's **Blarney Stone** probably won't give you good luck. In fact, it's situated in such an awkward position near the top of a very high wall that kissing it could lead to serious injury or even death.

Big Ben is not the name of the clock on the tower in London, or the tower itself. It's the name of the bell inside the tower.

The **Bridge of Sighs** in Venice, Italy was not given that name because of its reputation as a spot where young couples fall in love. It was originally a bridge to a horrible torture chamber. Convicts apparently sighed as they neared their fate.

London's **Buckingham Palace** is not owned by the British government. It's owned by Queen Elizabeth II and her family.

The eleven points on the maple leaf on the national flag of **Canada** do not represent the eleven provinces and territories of Canada. It just happened to end up that way.

The **Canary Islands** were not named for canaries. They were named for the wild dogs, or canines, that once lived there.

The **Cape of Good Hope** is not the southernmost tip of Africa. That distinction belongs to Cape Agulhas, which is 40 miles further south.

The **Caspian Sea** is not a sea. It's a lake. In fact, it's the largest lake in the world, and it has salt water. But it's still a lake.

Constantinople was not the original name for Istanbul, Turkey. Istanbul was the original name. The Romans called it Constantinople in honor of the emperor Constantine, but it was never a name used by the Turks.

The **Dead Sea** isn't a sea. It's a lake. And though fish and plants can't survive in its high salt content, microscopic bacteria and fungi do live there.

England is not a country. It's a political division inside the country called the United Kingdom.

The **Great Wall of China** cannot be seen from outer space. It's hard to say where that misconception came from since no astronaut has ever reported seeing it.

Greenland is not nearly as big as it looks on most maps. World maps tend to stretch out land masses nearer the poles. It's actually about the size of Alaska.

Greenland is not very green and **Iceland** is not very icy. Greenland is mostly covered by ice and Iceland is mostly covered by green vegetation.

Not all of the major mountains in the world have been climbed. **Khumba Yul Lha** in the Himalayans has not been climbed, not because it's particularly high or dangerous, but because climbing it is considered a religious taboo by the region's inhabitants.

There isn't just one **kremlin** in Russia. The Kremlin in Moscow is the biggest and most important, but many Russian cities have a walled fortress in the middle of town called a kremlin.

London is not a particularly rainy city. Though there is at least some rain on about 150 days a year, it's generally very light. London's annual rainfall of 24 inches makes it one of the driest places in Europe.

The bridge that was moved from London to Lake Havasu, Arizona is not the **London Bridge**. It was originally London's "Tower Bridge." Built in 1894, it is not the one in the very old song, "London Bridge is falling down…"

The world's tallest mountain measured from base to top is not **Mount Everest**. Mount Everest is indeed the highest mountain, but Hawaii's Mauna Kea is taller when you include the distance from the mountain's base on the ocean floor to the top of the ocean.

The **Netherlands** and Holland are not the same thing. The name of the country is The Netherlands. North Holland and South Holland are two of the country's twelve provinces.

When traveling from the Atlantic Ocean to the Pacific Ocean in the **Panama Canal**, you are not traveling west. You are traveling north. This is because of the way Panama is situated in Central America.

The locks used to raise ships in the **Panama Canal** aren't there because one of the oceans, the Atlantic or the Pacific, is higher than the other. It's because the canal travels up and over higher elevation land between the oceans.

Persia was not the original name for Iran. It's always been Iran. Persia was largely used by Westerners.

The world's largest **pyramids** are not in Egypt. They are in Mexico.

Moscow's **Red Square** did not receive that name because Communists lived there. It really is red and was red long before the Russian revolution.

Rome, known as the "City of Seven Hills," has considerably more than seven major hills. In fact, the hills listed among the seven have changed several times.

The **Sahara Desert** is not the world's biggest desert. That honor goes to the large desert in the interior of Antarctica.

Though **Switzerland** is famous for remaining neutral and avoiding participation in wars, that doesn't mean it doesn't have an army. In fact, Switzerland's army is one of the largest per capita.

Timbuktu is not a made-up place. It's a real city, and an important business center, in Africa's Republic of Mali.

Plant Life

Bamboo is not a type of tree. It's a type of grass that grows to tree-like heights.

The **Century Plant** doesn't take 100 years to bloom. In favorable climates, it blooms once every five to ten years.

Deciduous tree leaves don't "gain" color in the fall. They lose their green color, making the other colors visible.

The **Douglas fir** is not a fir tree. It belongs to a different genus known as Pseudotsuga.

Despite a popular idea in the 1960s, plants don't have **feelings**. No matter what you use, e.g., and EEG machine, no one has been able to show any sort of "feeling" occurring in a plant.

Flowers do not reduce the amount of oxygen in a hospital room. In fact, they give off more oxygen than they consume.

Spraying mist on **house plants** that normally thrive in humid climates has no impact. Occasional misting does not increase the humidity level. Nurseries sell indoor plants that can survive in a dry indoor climate.

That's not **moss** growing on the north side of your tree. Those are lichens. They are quite different—moss is a type of plant and lichens are a fungus.

Mushrooms are not plants. They are in a classification group separate from plants and animals called fungi.

Plant food is a misnomer. The minerals in these products are not really food for plants. "Fertilizer" is the better term.

Poinsettias are not poisonous to humans or their pets. They taste awful and may give you an upset stomach, but no one has ever died from this popular Christmas plant.

Not everyone will have an adverse reaction when they come in contact with **poison ivy**. Less than 50 percent of us will have a negative skin reaction when we touch it.

Poison ivy isn't ivy. It's a shrub unrelated to ivy.

Poison oak isn't oak. It isn't related to oak trees in any way.

Sagebrush is unrelated to the herb known as "sage." There is some similarity in terms of smell, but you wouldn't want the bitter-tasting sagebrush in any of your recipes.

That very sticky goo you find on your car when parked near a tree is probably not **sap** from the tree. It's generally the waste product of aphids and other bugs that have been feeding off the tree's leaves.

The **sequoia** trees found in California are not the world's tallest trees. That honor goes to giant eucalyptus trees in Australia. However, the California sequoias do have the greatest diameter.

The **tulip** did not originate in the Netherlands. It originated in Central Asia.

Many roses are red, but **violets** aren't blue. They're violet.

You can't water plants efficiently by pouring **water** over the leaves. Plants don't absorb water through their leaves. The water needs to get to the plant's roots. Only a relatively small portion of the water may get to the roots if you water in this manner.

Religion

Allah is not a Muslim god that is distinct from the Christian version. It is just the Arabic word for "God." Arabic-speaking Christians refer to God as "Allah."

Though paintings typically depict **angels** as winged females, the Bible never mentions angel wings and refers to most angels as males.

A.D. does not stand for "After Death." It stands for **Anno Domini**, which means "In the year of the Lord." It indicates the approximate number of years since Christ's birth.

Though the book **The Bible Code** argues there is a hidden code in the Bible that accurately predicts future events, the analysis is flawed. The same sort of analysis applied to other books provides similar results, e.g., Moby Dick predicts the assassination of Martin Luther King.

Buddha is not the name for God in Buddhism. The name means "enlightened one" and originally referred to a prince named Siddhartha Gautama. Followers can theoretically become a Buddha by obtaining full enlightenment.

It is not a rule **Catholic priests** must be unmarried. The rule is they can't marry while a priest. There are some Catholic priests who were married before they were ordained.

The **cross** symbol used in Christianity is not the same shape as the cross Christ died on. Roman crucifixions took place on a T-shaped cross.

The Bible doesn't say anything about Mary riding a **donkey** to Bethlehem. It only mentions she traveled with Joseph and says nothing about her mode of transportation.

A **fatwa** is not a death sentence. It's a religious opinion issued by an Islamic scholar. The misconception is a result of Ayatollah Khomeini's particular fatwa calling for the death of author Salman Rushdie.

The Bible never states it was an apple that was eaten in the **Garden of Eden**. It simply states it was the "fruit of the tree." For that matter, experts agree apples never grew in the region where Eden would have existed.

Good Friday, the commemoration of Jesus's death, did not receive that name because of anything "good" that happened. Good was once a variation of God, similar to the way "good-bye" comes from "God be with you."

The **Immaculate Conception** does not refer to the virgin birth of Christ. It's the belief Mary, mother of Jesus, was born without original sin.

The Bible never refers to **Mary Magdalene** as a prostitute. At one point, it mentions she was possessed by "seven demons," but it is unclear what that means.

Though the Bible says **Methuselah** lived to be 969, he's not the oldest person mentioned. According to the Bible, Methuselah's father, Enoch, would never die. That would make him about 5,400 years old at this point.

Money is the root of all evil is not the correct passage in the Bible. It's actually "For the love of money is the root of all evil." It's an obsession with money, not money itself, which leads to problems.

Muslims do not pray to **Muhammad**. Muhammad is considered a prophet, not a god. Muslims pray to Allah.

Most **Muslims** are not Arabs. Only one-fifth of all Muslims are Arabic. Most Muslims live in India, Indonesia, or one of the other Asian countries east of Arabic populations.

The **number of the beast**, according to the Bible, is not 666. That number comes from an incorrect translation. The earliest known copy of the Book of Revelation shows it to be 616.

There is no book called **Revelations** in the Bible. It's called Revelation.

Churches do not ask people refrain to from throwing **rice** at weddings because it can make birds sick. Rice does not make birds sick. Churches ask rice not be thrown because of the possible liability if anyone at the wedding slipped on the rice.

In the Bible, Delilah does not cut **Samson**'s hair. She orders someone else to do it.

There is no single consistent set of **Ten Commandments**. They vary across versions of the Bible.

There weren't necessarily **three wise men** who visited the baby Jesus in the manger. The Bible says nothing about how many there were. The common assumption is three because the wise men brought three gifts: gold, frankincense, and myrrh. In addition, the Bible says the Magi visited Jesus as a child, which could have been several months or years after his birth.

The Qur'an, Islam's holy book, does not say heroes will be greeted by 72 **virgins** when they get to heaven. Translators now believe the passage refers to rare fruit, specifically white raisins, found in a lush garden of pools and trees.

Jesus was not born in the **year zero**. Nor was anyone else. When modern calendars were created to reflect the birth of Christ, AD 1 directly followed the year 1 BC. Jesus's actual birth year has never been verified—the best guesses are somewhere between 6 and 4 B.C.

Science and Technology

Not all scientists are **atheists**. In fact, about half report they believe in God.

Not all **bacteria** are bad. In fact, the vast majority play a harmless or even important role, such as aiding the digestive system, fighting off viruses, and decomposing dead plants and animals.

It's not **centrifugal force** that pushes you outward when sitting in a rotating carnival ride. It's "inertia" that pushes your body away from the center of the ride.

Turning a light off and on does not use a substantial amount of **electricity**. A common belief is it's better to leave a light on than turn it off for a short time, e.g., 30 minutes. In truth, the flick of a light switch is equivalent to less than a second of light. It's much better to turn a light off when leaving the room, even if you plan to return just minutes later.

Ancient Egyptians didn't have special **embalming** secrets. Mummies lasted longer from that area because of the unusually dry climate and relative absence of bacteria in the air and sand.

Evolution theory does not state humans evolved from apes. It says humans and apes evolved from a common ancestor.

Evolution theory does not state species necessarily "improve" over time. Some species, e.g., sharks, stay the same. Others adapt, but have their environment subsequently altered, leaving their condition worse.

The hottest part of a **fire** is not inside the fire. It's right above the fire.

Glass is not a liquid. Supposedly, glass continues to move at a very slow rate over time. One alleged proof is that older panes of glass tend to be thicker on the bottom. In fact, if a glass pane is thicker at the bottom, it must have occurred during the manufacturing process.

Ice is not slippery. Ice becomes slippery only when the surface layer thaws and a fine film of water forms over the top.

The **law of averages** does not predict an event is more likely to happen after a long stretch of it not happening. Say a tossed coin is heads ten consecutive times. The law of averages does not say it is more likely to be tails on the eleventh toss. It's still only a 50% chance it will come up tails. The law only states that, in the long run, cumulated results will tend closer to the average.

A **light-year** is not a measure of time. It's a measure of distance. It's the distance a ray of light will travel in one year.

Natural gas has no odor. An odorant is added so leaks can be more easily detected.

The **octane level** of gasoline has nothing to do with the power or performance of your car's engine. It is only an indicator of the gasoline's anti-knock resistance.

The **Pasteurization process** does not kill all bacteria. In fact, Pasteurization is performed at a fairly low temperature—well below boiling. The process, however, does kill the most dangerous bacteria.

A **quantum leap** is not a very big shift in something. Quantum physics describes very small things. A quantum leap would be a very small shift.

The white cloud produced by a steam plant or a teapot is not **steam**. Steam is invisible. It's vapor created as the steam cools and condenses.

Tear gas is not a gas. It's a chemical compound that produces gas-like vapors upon dispersal.

In science, the word **theory** does not suggest doubt about the validity of the theory, similar to the way a detective might have a "theory" about who committed a crime. A scientific theory is a set of principles which explain observations in nature. The principles of the theories of relativity and evolution, for example, are not in doubt.

Pure **water** is not a good conductor of electricity. However, water does conduct electricity in many situations, e.g., a bathtub, because it often contains minerals that allow good electrical conduction.

Space

Neil Armstrong wasn't supposed to say, as he stepped onto the moon's surface, "That's one small step for man, one giant leap for mankind." He was supposed to say, "That's one small step for a man, one giant leap for mankind." He apparently botched the line during all the excitement.

Unlike scenes from sci-fi movies, flying through an **asteroid belt** would not be particularly tricky. The average distance between asteroids that could cause damage is 1.25 million miles.

Black holes do not pull objects toward them any more than any other star. Their gravitational pull is identical to other stars.

A **blue moon** is not when the moon appears to be blue. It's the somewhat rare occurrence of two full moons in the same month. Smoke and dust particles in the atmosphere can sometimes make the moon appear blue; however, this is unrelated to how often a full moon appears in a month.

A **comet's tail** does not always follow the comet as it travels through the sky. Sometimes it's in front. The comet's tail always points away from the sun. Sunlight vaporizes parts of the comet and causes a dust and ion tail.

Constellations don't appear in the same place in the sky through the night. All stars, except Polaris—the North Star—change locations in the sky as the Earth rotates.

There is no **dark side of the moon**, i.e., a side that never sees daylight. While only one side of the moon ever faces Earth (because of gravitational pull), the "far side" of the moon faces the sun no less than the side facing us.

Lunar and solar **eclipses** are not that rare—each occurs a few times per year. Total solar eclipses are rarer, and seem especially rare because they can only be seen from a relatively small portion of the Earth's surface.

110

The **Evening Star** is not a star and doesn't only appear in the evening. It's the planet Venus, and is also known as the "Morning Star" when it's visible in the early morning.

The United States was not **first to the moon**. The Soviet Union landed an unmanned ship on the moon in 1959—ten years before the Apollo 11 landing.

Sir Edmund Halley did not discover Halley's Comet. Astronomers knew about the comet before Halley was born. It was named for Halley after he correctly predicted it would return every 76 years.

Though closest to the sun, **Mercury** is not the hottest planet. Because its dense atmosphere traps the Sun's heat, Venus is the hottest planet.

Despite racing through the Earth's atmosphere at high temperatures, **meteors** are not hot when they strike the earth as meteorites. They are often cool to the touch.

The phrase, **meteoric rise**, referring to folks who have made a quick rise to fame, is incorrect. Meteors fall, not rise.

It's not always cold on the **moon**. While temperatures can dip as low as -387 degrees Fahrenheit, they can also go as high as 253 degrees on the side facing the sun.

The **phases of the moon** are not a result of the Earth's shadow on the moon. That's what happens in a lunar eclipse. The phase of the moon is dictated by how much of the moon is facing the sun on a given night. When the moon is at a right angle from the sun (relative to the Earth), we only see about half of the lighted surface, creating a "half moon."

Polaris, aka the "North Star," is not the brightest star in the sky. That honor goes to Sirius.

Saturn is not the only planet in our solar system with rings. Jupiter, Uranus, and Neptune also have rings. The rings around those planets just aren't as bright.

Shooting stars, i.e., meteors, are not only not stars, they are usually very small. Many are the size of a pebble.

There are not nine planets in our **solar system**. Pluto was officially demoted to a "dwarf planet" in 2006 by the International Astronomers Union.

Stars really don't twinkle. They only appear to twinkle because their light is passing through moving layers of atmosphere over the earth. Stars appear to be a steady point of light to astronauts in space.

The **stars** you see at night don't necessarily exist. Many are thousands, even millions, of light-years away, so we're seeing them as they were thousands or millions of years ago. Many of the stars we can see may now be dead.

While it was established long ago that the Earth orbits around the **sun**, that doesn't mean the sun is stationary. It both rotates on its axis and orbits around the center of the Milky Way galaxy.

Though the **sun and the moon** appear to be the same size, they are not. It's a coincidence the sun is both 400 times bigger than the moon, and 400 times farther away than the moon.

Looking at a **total solar eclipse** will not damage your eyes. If the eclipse is indeed total, then there are no sun rays that can cause damage. Remember, though, even a short glimpse at a partial eclipse can permanently injure your eyes.

Sports

Abbott and Costello were never inducted into baseball's Hall of Fame. A recording of their "Who's on First" routine is often played, but that's as close as they came.

The largest prize in yacht racing, the **America's Cup**, was not named in honor of the United States of America. It was named after a historic yacht named "America."

The Yankees did not design pinstriped uniforms to disguise **Babe Ruth's** weight problem. Like many other teams, they used pinstriped uniforms before the Babe arrived.

Basketball rims are not just slightly wider than basketballs. The width of a basketball rim is 18 inches, while a basketball is just a little more than half of that.

A **black belt** in martial arts does not necessarily indicate mastery. It indicates competence of all the basic techniques. Various black belt levels indicate whether one is a master or grandmaster.

In **bullfighting**, the bull is not particularly angry because the matador's cape is red. Bulls are colorblind. They just don't like silly little capes being waved in their face.

Fidel Castro never had a tryout with the Washington Senators baseball team. He enjoyed playing baseball in Cuba, but was never a Major League Baseball prospect.

Corked baseball bats do no make the ball go farther. In fact, scientific tests show a ball struck with a corked bat goes less distance than a ball hit with a fully wooden bat.

Abner Doubleday didn't invent baseball. The process was too gradual for any single person to get credit, though a fellow named Alexander Cartwright made the most substantial contributions. The claim that Doubleday was the inventor was a publicity stunt to bring tourists to his hometown of Cooperstown.

The **foul pole and foul line** in baseball are not in foul territory. They are in fair territory. If the ball touches either one, it is considered a fair ball.

The **golf clubs** known as "woods" are generally not made of wood. They generally consist of metal or composite materials.

Strictly speaking, you're not playing at **golf links** unless you're near the water. To a Scotsman, "links" refers to the seashore. Golf links are courses located on sandy, seaside property.

The **Harlem Globetrotters** basketball team is not, and has never been, based in Harlem. The team originated in Chicago.

No little boy said, "Say it ain't so, Joe" to baseball player **Shoeless Joe Jackson** after the 1919 Chicago Black Sox story broke. It was made up by a sports writer.

The story about two men blowing up their dog and truck while **ice fishing** is not true. Supposedly, their loyal dog retrieved a thrown stick of dynamite and hid under their truck. This story is an urban legend.

Ice hockey is not the official national sport of Canada. That honor goes to lacrosse. For what it's worth, ice hockey is Canada's official national winter sport.

Karate did not originate in Japan. It originated in India and didn't catch on in Japan until many years later.

Green Bay Packers coach **Vince Lombardi** did not say, "Winning isn't everything, it's the only thing." The quote is from a 1953 John Wayne film called "Trouble along the Way." However, Lombardi, did say, "Winning isn't everything, but wanting to win is."

Not every football player who appeared on the cover of the **Madden NFL** video game played poorly in the subsequent year. Although several players had injury-riddled seasons, this is a relatively common occurrence in the NFL.

A **marathon** is not 26.2 miles because that's the distance from Marathon to Athens in Greece. That distance is 21.4 miles. The distance of the race was stretched over time. The last adjustment occurred at the 1908 London Olympics, when the British royal family insisted the race begin at Windsor Castle and finish in front of the royal box at the Olympic Stadium.

The **New York** Jets and New York Giants don't play in New York. They play in New Jersey.

Men weren't the only ones who won events in the ancient Greek **Olympics**. While women weren't allowed to watch the Olympics, a woman named Kyniska was credited with winning a chariot race. She was given the medal because she was the breeder of the horse that won. The chariot drivers were slaves and were not given credit for the victory.

The 1988 Seoul **Olympics** were not the first to allow professional athletes. Most athletes in the ancient Olympics received prizes from their home cities for winning.

Olympic medals haven't been given out only for athletic endeavors. At the 1912 Stockholm games, medals were given for writing, architecture, sculpture, painting, and music.

The story that 1936 Olympics track star **Jesse Owens** was snubbed by Adolph Hitler is not true. The apparently-bored Hitler left the Olympic Games after the first day and wasn't around to award any winners, whether they were black, white, American, or German.

In baseball, a player's **on-base percentage** is not a percentage. It's presented as a three-place decimal average, e.g., .325. A percentage in this example would be 32.5%.

Footballs are not **pigskins**. They are made from cowhide.

The name of the game with paddles and a little white plastic ball is not **Ping Pong**. The actual name is table tennis. Ping Pong is a trademarked name used by one manufacturer.

Jackie Robinson was not the first black player in major league baseball. Fleet Walker was the first in the 1880s. A ban was established after Walker played and didn't end until Robinson's debut in 1947.

The **San Diego Chargers** football team was not named the Chargers because they ran fast with the ball. The name came from the team's first owner, Barron Hilton, who owned a credit card company.

Skier **Picabo Street** was never banned from answering the phone while working in a hospital as a nurse. Because her first name is pronounced "peek-a-boo," she supposedly upset folks when she answered the phone, "Picabo, I.C.U." This just originated from a funny joke—Picabo Street has never been a nurse.

Having **sex** before a sporting event does not negatively affect an athlete's performance. Studies have shown that recently active athletes do just as well.

Not all athletes who appear on the cover of **Sports Illustrated** have been jinxed. Michael Jordan appeared a record 49 times and never seemed to have a problem.

There is no evidence any city's sewage system was ever backed up because of the high number of toilet flushes at halftime of the **Super Bowl**. Apparently, viewers spread their toilet visits throughout the game.

The incidence of domestic abuse is no higher on **Super Bowl** Sundays. This is one of those myths that started with a few anecdotal incidents and grew into a supposed fact.

In baseball, there's no rule that says **tie goes to the runner**. Umpires are expected to decide which arrived first: the ball or the runner.

The **Washington Wizards** basketball team doesn't play in Washington, D.C. or Washington State. They play in Maryland.

Baseball's **World Series** was not named for the New York World, a popular newspaper when the series was first played. It really did imply the winners were the champions of the world.

Television

Barry Williams and Florence Henderson, the actors who played Greg and his mother Carol on **The Brady Bunch**, did not have an affair during the filming of the show. However, they did go on one date.

"Tonight Show" host **Johnny Carson** didn't ask Arnold Palmer's wife if she had a pre-tournament ritual, to which she supposedly replied, "Yes, I kiss his balls for good luck." It was just part of a joke that folks started to believe was true.

Dragnet's Sgt. Joe Friday, played by Jack Webb, never said, "Just the facts, ma'am." The closest he ever came was "All we want are the facts, ma'am."

Fred and Wilma **Flintstone** were not the first TV couple to share a bed. Nor was it the Munsters or the Bradys—other famous couples rumored to be first. The first were the lead characters in a forgotten 1947 sitcom called "Mary Kay and Johnny."

After a woman explained she was the mother of ten children because she loved her husband, "You Bet Your Life" host **Groucho Marx** did not respond, "I love my cigar, too, but I take it out of my mouth once in a while." Groucho, among others, said none of this story ever occurred.

Vivian Vance was not contractually obligated to be overweight while she was a co-star on **I Love Lucy**. Her character, Ethel Mertz, was dressed and made up to look older and less attractive than Lucy, but the contract story is a myth.

Iron Eyes Cody, the actor who played a crying Indian in the famous **Keep America Beautiful** ad about pollution, was not an Indian. He was an Italian named Oscar DeCorti.

The "actors" who portrayed **Lassie** in the 1950s and 1960s TV show were not females. Male collies were always used because they tend to shed less.

Jerry Mathers, child star of **Leave It to Beaver**, was not killed in Vietnam. He's still alive—often seen in "Leave It to Beaver" sequels and various tribute shows.

Little Mikey, the boy in the **Life Cereal** commercial, did not die from consuming a combination of pop rocks and Coke. Not only is the man who played Mikey still alive today, but nobody has ever died from a combination of pop rocks and Coke.

The death of Colonel Blake in **M*A*S*H** was not kept a secret from the other cast members to heighten the emotional impact during filming. Though the cast was surprised when they read the script, they knew what was going to happen while the cameras rolled.

Fred Rogers, the star of **Mr. Rogers' Neighborhood**, did not wear a long sleeve sweater to hide tattoos from his days as a sniper in the Vietnam War. He had no tattoos, and was too old to have served in the Vietnam War.

No character said, "Oh no, Mr. Bill!" in the series of **Saturday Night Live** short films. Mr. Bill was the name of the clay character who said, "Oh no!" as he was subjected to various indignities by an off-screen man known as Mr. Hands.

Soupy Sales never told dirty jokes on his popular children's show. For years, Sales offered $10,000 to anyone could find any evidence of him telling a dirty joke on the air, and he never had to pay up.

Star Trek's Captain Kirk, played by William Shatner, never said "Beam me up, Scotty." The closest he came was "Beam me up, Mr. Scott."

Star Trek's Dr. McCoy, played by Deforest Kelly, never said, "Damn it, Jim! I'm a doctor not a..." At the time of the series, "damn" was a swear word that could not be used on TV.

George Reeves, the actor who portrayed **Superman** in the 50s television series, did not die when he jumped off a building thinking he was superman. He was shot in the head, with some controversy over whether it was suicide or murder.

World History

Marie Antoinette never said, "Let them eat cake." It was originally credited to the Duchess of Tuscany long before Marie Antoinette's time. The quote was used by her opposition to discredit her.

Julius Caesar likely did not say, "Et tu, Brute." Historians at the time said he said nothing at his assassination. The phrase was invented by Shakespeare for his play about Julius Caesar.

Julius Caesar was never emperor of Rome. He was a general and statesman who was eventually appointed dictator. The first Roman emperor was his successor, Augustus Caesar.

Several Roman emperors were named **Caesar**, yet none were direct descendents of their predecessors. Instead, the current Caesar gave his name to his successor by officially adopting him.

Early humans weren't really **cavemen**. The usually lived in huts and tents, and only used caves for ritual ceremonies.

Chemical warfare did not originate during World War I. Alexander the Great used lime to make his enemies itch in the 4th century B.C. In the 17th century, the Spanish used smoke bombs.

There's no evidence **Christians** were ever thrown to the lions during the Roman Empire, or any other time.

Denmark's **King Christian X** did not thwart the Nazi's attempts to identify Jews by wearing a yellow star himself. Danish Jews were never forced to wear the Star of David.

Cleopatra's death was probably not the result of an asp bite. There were no asps in Egypt at the time of Cleopatra. If she did die from a snake bite, it was probably a cobra.

Captain Cook's 1770 exploration of Australia was not the first visit by a European. Dutch visitors arrived more than 100 years earlier.

Contrary to a poem by John Keats, **Hernando Cortez** was not the first European to see the Pacific Ocean. It was Vasco Balboa. Cortez's "claim to fame" was the decimation of the Aztecs in Mexico.

When Spanish conquerors first began searching for **El Dorado**, they were not looking for a golden city. "El Dorado" originally referred to a golden man. They believed there was a ruler whose body was covered with a paste of gold dust. The story eventually expanded to the ruler's golden city.

Medieval people did not believe the world was **flat**. It was common knowledge at the time the Earth was round. People had observed eclipses for thousands of years and understood the Earth was a round object. Apparently, the whole idea stems from a mostly false biography of Christopher Columbus written by Washington Irving.

The explorer **Henry Hudson** did not discover Hudson Bay. It was just named for him. It's not known for sure which European first visited this body of water, but a Portuguese explorer named Estevan Gomez was there in 1525—approximately 40 years before Hudson was born.

Lady Godiva was a real person, but there's no evidence she rode naked through town on a horse. The story didn't first appear until well over 200 years after her death.

The dropping of the atomic bomb on **Hiroshima**, which killed 75,000, was not the deadliest attack of World War II. Over 135,000 died when Dresden, Germany was fire bombed and approximately 85,000 died when napalm was dropped on Tokyo.

Ferdinand Magellan was not the first man to sail around the world. His ships returned to Spain in 1522 after a complete trip, but he wasn't aboard. He was killed in 1521 in the Philippines.

King John did not sign the **Magna Carta** in 1215. He didn't know how to write. The document was made official when his royal seal was attached.

The oldest **mummy** every found was not Egyptian. A mummy of a man believed to have died around 5000 B.C. was found in Chile—more than 2000 years older than the oldest Egyptian mummy.

Benito Mussolini did not make the Italian trains run on time. The government improved most of the bad situation before Mussolini's Fascist regime came to power. Plus those who lived through the era say the railway's ability to run on time was generally exaggerated.

The emperor **Nero** did not play a fiddle as Rome burned. There were no fiddles at that time. In fact, Nero did his best to organize a response to the fire, including help for the homeless.

The **100-Year War** was not 100 years long. It lasted 116 years.

Contrary to biblical movies, the laborers who built the **pyramids** were generally not slaves. Recent excavations indicate the workers were well paid Egyptian citizens.

Sir Walter Raleigh did not drape his cloak over a puddle so Queen Elizabeth I could avoid soiling her queenly garb. It was completely made up by a truth-stretching historian by the name of Thomas Fuller.

According to most calendars, the **Russian October Revolution** did not start in October. It started on November 7, 1917. At the time, Russia was still using the Julian calendar (unlike most of the world), and it indicated October 25. The revolutionaries, only six months later, changed to the Gregorian calendar, which moved the date to November.

Though the **Spanish Armada** was known as one of the most powerful naval forces ever, it was soundly defeated in its only battle. In 1588, the British navy did not lose a single ship as they virtually sank the Armada in the North Sea.

Historians are reasonably sure **Spartacus** was not killed by crucifixion, as depicted in the movie. He was probably killed in battle.

Ancient Romans did not signal for the death of a gladiator with a **thumbs-down** signal. The actual gesture for death included the thumb pointing inward, like a dagger thrust.

Nothing in the **tombs of ancient Egyptian pharaohs** suggests those who enter the tomb will be cursed. The idea was invented by Jane Loudon Webb in her 1828 book <u>The Mummy</u>.

If there was a **Trojan horse**, it wasn't created by the Trojans. The story of the Trojan horse describes the trick used by Greek soldiers to get past the wall that surrounded the City of Troy.

King Tut's tomb was not the most elaborate ever. It's just that it was well preserved. Archeologists believe King Tutankhamen was not an important pharaoh, and his tomb was relatively minor compared to other pharaohs.

Vikings warriors did not wear horned helmets. They were used in Celtic religious ceremonies, but there was no practical reason for warriors to wear awkward headgear of this type.

Napoleon Bonaparte's decisive defeat wasn't in **Waterloo**. The Battle of Waterloo was fought in the nearby town of Pancenoit.

www.ingramcontent.com/pod-product-compliance
Lightning Source LLC
Chambersburg PA
CBHW020259290526
45784CB00003B/1296